Testimony
Volume 1:
Alien Abduction in the UK

Andy Russell

Copyright © 2024 Andy Russell

All rights reserved.

CONTENTS

	Introduction	i
1	A Very Brief History	Pg 1
2	A Very British Abduction	Pg 15
3	A Sceptical Viewpoint	Pg 31
4	The Problem with Hypnosis	Pg 46
5	Alien Abduction: The Overview	Pg 58
6	Case Study #1 - Mike	Pg 62
7	Case Study #2 - Tina	Pg 72
8	Case Study #3 - Marcie	Pg 85
9	Case Study #4 - Nika	Pg 96
10	Case Study #5 - Jana	Pg 114

INTRODUCTION

"I was suddenly very aware that I was now back in my bedroom. The return to the reality that I recognized was so mentally jarring in comparison to finding myself unable to move on a cold examination table surrounded by unusual creatures. The alarm clock rang, I almost jumped a mile, the everyday reality was now bursting into life. My husband was stirring, the kids were getting ready for school, I had work to think about so all I could do was focus on the Monday morning unfolding before me and hope that I could get time to deal with these weird incidents later."

Linzy began to sob into her hands, the enormity of her stories finally came crashing down on top of her. We had listened in silence as she had explained her life of abduction incidents. We had seen her turn crimson with embarrassment as she related the intimate parts of her examinations at the hands of her alien captors. The other abductees in the group offered words of sympathy and exchanged knowing looks. Linzy's experiences solidified the others in their beliefs.

*

Starting in the 1980s and 1990s there was a sudden rise in stories of alien abduction, and whilst many within UFOlogy were aware of the phenomena, these stories of alien abduction were now breaking into mainstream awareness. As I revisited a lot of these cases I wondered what the state of the UK abduction community was currently. After the heyday of the 1980s/1990s, the abduction phenomena appeared to have retreated into the shadows. The research seemed to have ground to a halt, with both believers and sceptics entrenched in their respective positions.

During the mid to late 1990s I had encountered many abductees and had kept in touch with a large portion of them. Many of the abductees I had met had never used hypnosis and had many vivid memories to furnish their belief that they had been abducted by aliens and believed these abductions had taken place for a seemingly large range of different agendas.

In the early 2000's I trained for a year as a clinical hypnotherapist & psychotherapist. I soon learned that the reliance on hypnosis to further abduction research was potentially floored. Plus, to the casual observer of the literature, it really appeared that there were very few people actually assisting abductees, instead opting to treat them as raw material for the next book. Not only that, but there was also little research challenging the accepted parameters of the phenomena as set out by the leading lights of the abduction research community. What was defined in the "classic era" of the phenomena has always been accepted by believers despite the advances in science that may indicate the phenomena is not what we thought it could be. But those who were at the centre of the phenomena, the abductees/experiencers, they always seemed to fade into the background, their voices often filtered through the researcher. So where were they now? Where is the subject now, in terms of its understanding?

Over the years, I have met with and discussed the phenomena with around 350 abductees/experiencers. I have regularly attended various abductee/experiencer support groups purely as an observer. As the topic of UFO/UAP disclosure is once again being discussed at the highest levels of the US government, now more than any other time we need to listen to the voices of abductees & experiencers.

1 A VERY BRIEF HISTORY

Despite what pop-culture might tell you, alien abductions did not start in the 1980s although it might have felt like it at the time. It certainly rose in media and cultural visibility during the 1980s and 1990s, but its roots go much further back. In fact, its roots go way back into history and probably due to the lack of suitable language at the time, many such abduction encounters were dismissed or described in a manner suitable to the time it was experienced, such as encounters with fairies or other-worldly beings or demons[1].

One of the reasons I wanted to look at some aspects of the history of abduction is that the earlier accounts have a certain naïve authenticity that I think is important. We also see some themes start to develop in the earlier cases that are regularly present in many of the more famous or recent cases. The foundations of the modern abduction phenomena are laid down in these early cases.

This is just an overview of these cases as many of them are extremely complex and are worth a more in-depth appraisal. Certainly, cases

---

[1] In 2004 I met an Irish farmer who claimed to have been "fairied" on his own land. He claimed that he met two "little people" in one of his fields, as he was checking the fences. He claimed that he had about an hour of missing time he could not account for. The farmer also claimed he was disorientated for a while after his encounter, failing to recognise his own land and his own house. His family confirmed that he eventually returned to the farmhouse in a disorientated state, struggling to formulate coherent sentences and was extremely agitated for a few hours after the incident.

such as those of Betty and Barney Hill or the Linda Cortile case are rabbit holes that have kept people searching for many, many years.

There are some very early cases that appear to be abduction-like encounters that have been well documented and researcher Jerome Clark has labelled these as 'paleo-abductions'[2]. In 1897, Colonel H. G. Shaw claimed that he and a friend were harassed by three tall, slender humanoids whilst out driving. Shaw claimed that whilst driving through countryside, near Stockton, he came across what appeared to be a spacecraft that had landed. Shaw claimed that three, hairless, slender aliens, all approaching 7 foot in height, started to inspect the buggy he and his friend were riding in. The three aliens tried to force Shaw and his companion onto the ship, but Shaw and his friend were able to fight his would-be abductors off. This is believed by many to be the first published story of an attempted alien abduction.

In the same year as Colonel Shaw's incident, a story was published in the *Table Rock Argus* which documented how a group of witnesses saw a mysterious airship sailing overhead (The witnesses were described as "anonymous but reliable"). The occupants of the airship were visible to the witnesses, who also saw a woman who had evidently been captured and tied to a chair, whilst being tended to by another woman and watched over by a man with a pistol.

Paris Match is a weekly French language news magazine, which in 1954, ran the story of an incident that occurred in 1921. The writer, who remained anonymous, detailed his experience as a child of being snatched by two tall "men" who wore strange helmets and "diving suits" who took him to an "odd shaped tank". The men soon released him after he became understandably upset.

These early accounts lack a lot of detail but provide an interesting insight to the early reports of potential alien abduction. As time moved on, the reports became a lot more detailed, which only added to the questions around the phenomena.

Antonia Vilas-Boas

---

[2] Colvin, T. "UFOs And Fairies/Legends/Supernatural – Pt. I"

The first 'classic' alien abduction report came from a 23-year-old Brazilian farmer named Antonio Vilas-Boas and predates the Betty & Barney Hill incident by several years. On October 16, 1957, Antonio was ploughing fields at night to avoid the intense temperatures of the day. Antonio became aware of what he thought was a red star. The object started to approach Antonio, who could now see that it was a circular or egg-shaped object. The object had a red light at the front of the craft and a rotating dome on top. As the object got close to Antonio he decided to flee on his tractor, but the tractor soon lost power. Fleeing on foot, Antonio was soon grabbed by a tall humanoid who was wearing grey overalls and a helmet. Antonio explained that the humanoids he subsequently witnessed in the craft were small, blue and made strange barks or yelps, which he assumed was some form of communication.

Once on board, Antonio's clothes were removed, and his body was covered all-over with a gel-like substance. Antonio was led to a room where samples of his blood were taken. Antonio was then led to another room where he was left for around 30 minutes. In this room, a gas soon started to emanate which made Antonio feel ill. After another short time, Antonio was joined in the room by another being who was female. This being was the same height as the others and had a pointed chin with large cat-like eyes. Her hair was white, but her armpit and pubic hair were bright blood red. Antonio felt strongly attracted to the woman and they subsequently had sex.

Once intercourse was over, the being rubbed her stomach and pointed to the sky, which Antonio felt meant that she was going to raise their child in space. Antonio was given back his clothes and was given a brief tour of the ship. On the tour Antonio tried to steal a clock-like device from the craft but was prevented from doing so. Antonio was escorted off the craft and watched as it rose skyward. On returning to his home, Antonio was astonished to find four hours had passed. Antonio suffered from nausea, general weakness/fatigue, and headaches after the event. This event happened several years before the famous Betty and Barney Hill encounter and already we can see the most common stages of most abduction stories are in place: the abduction, medical exam, sexual liaison, tour of the craft, missing time, and a general unwell feeling.

Despite occurring before the famous Betty and Barny Hill experience, the Vila-Boas incident was not widely publicised until after the Hill's experience which rules out the Hill's borrowing elements of previous stories, as suggested by sceptics, to concoct a similar story. It is also worth noting that Antonio did not have to recover any of these memories via hypnosis.

Betty & Barney Hill

The Hill's encounter took place on September 19, 1961, as they were driving back to Portsmouth having just vacationed in Niagara Falls and Montreal. As the couple drove south of Lancaster, New Hampshire, Betty claimed she watched a bright point of light that moved from below the moon. Betty thought she was observing a falling star but decided against that notion when she saw the light start to move upward. The light started to move more erratically and was starting to get closer to the Hill's position. Betty made Barney pull over to observe the light and from the picnic area south of Twin Mountain they watched the "odd-shaped" craft through binoculars.

Extremely unnerved, the Hill's got back into the car and continued driving. The object continued to move erratically in the sky as the Hill's drove on. It was not until the couple approached Indian Head did the situation start to escalate. The object suddenly and rapidly descended towards the vehicle causing Barney to stop the car in the middle of the road. The silent craft hovered around 80-100 feet above the car. Barney jumped out of the car whilst Betty remained inside looking at the object through binoculars. Betty claimed to have witnessed between 8 to 11 figures looking out of the craft's windows. Barney ran back to the car in almost hysterics stating that, "They're going to capture us!"

Once in the car, Barney sped away whilst Betty kept looking at the object. Both claimed to have started to hear rhythmical beeping noises, and both felt the car seem to vibrate with the tingling sensation passing through their bodies. The Hill's claimed that they soon entered an altered state of consciousness which left their mental faculties feeling dulled. Another set of beeping noises soon brought the Hill's back to full consciousness. They found they had travelled almost 35 miles in what seemed like seconds, but they also had hazy recollections of the journey. They also recalled making an unplanned, sudden turn and encountered a roadblock and witnessing a fiery orb in the road.

The Hill's arrived home around dawn, feeling slightly disoriented and displaying odd behaviour. They also noted odd things such as the torn binocular strap but could not remember it tearing. They also noticed their watches had stopped and would not restart. Barney's shoes were also showing signs of being scuffed and scraped but they did not know why that should be so.

Despite the strange immediate after-effects of the encounter, it was not until ten days after the encounter that Betty had any meaningful recollections of the events. Just after the incident, both Betty and Barney found it difficult to remember the events of that night. They complained of a mental fog when trying to piece together what happened, but for five successive nights Betty had vivid dreams about the incident. In one of the dreams Betty claims that she was forced by two small men to walk into the forest at night. She saw Barney and called out to him, but Barney seemed to be in a trance or altered state. The men were around five feet tall and wore matching blue uniforms. They appeared to be nearly human, with black hair, dark eyes, prominent noses, and bluish lips. Their skin was grey in colour.

The dream continued with both Betty and Barney walking up a ramp onto a metallic-looking disc-shaped craft. Once inside the craft, Betty and Barney were separated. A man approached Betty to carry out a physical examination. Betty claimed that the "examiner" was pleasant enough, but his grasp of English was poor, and she had difficulty understanding what he was saying. The examiner explained to Betty that he wanted to see the difference between humans and the occupants of the craft. The examiner conducted what would pass as a typical medical examination, checking Betty's eyes, ears, mouth, teeth before taking trimmings from her fingernails. After moving the examination on to Betty's legs and feet, the examiner took a sample of Betty's skin. The examiner then put a needle into Betty's navel, which she found excruciatingly painful, but the examiner waved his hand in front of her eyes and Betty felt the pain disappear.

Once the examination was over the examiner left the room and Betty started to converse with the being she felt was the leader. Betty asked the leader where they had come from. The leader pulled down a map and explained where they had originated from. A copy of the map that Betty had subsequently drawn appeared in *Interrupted Journey* (John Fuller's book on the Hill's experience).

In 1968 Marjorie Fish, an elementary teacher and amateur astronomer, decided to see if she could decipher Betty's star map, as depicted in Fuller's book. Marjorie assumed that one of the points on the map must represent the Sun, and finally deduced through creating three-dimensional models and observing distances based on the 1969 Gliese Star Catalogue, that the star map must represent the double star system of Zeta Reticuli. The validity of the star map continues to be argued over[3].

The Hill's were soon led down the ramp and they were advised to watch the craft depart, which they duly did. The Hills then returned to their car and resumed their journey.

It took hypnotic regression for Barney to come to terms and relay the events of that night. Barney explained that he and Betty were taken onto the craft where they were separated from each other. Barney was led onto a rectangular table but by Barney's own admission he kept his eyes closed for most of the examination. A cup-like device was placed over Barney's genitals which Barney believed took a semen sample. Barney also claimed that he had a thin tube or cylindrical device briefly placed in his anus. Barney also remembered watching the craft depart.

Under hypnosis, Betty's account was like that of her dreams but there were some discernible differences. The differences were mainly around the capture and release of the Hills. There were also some differences around the technology and the physical appearance of the craft's occupants.

Dr. Benjamin Simon, a Boston psychiatrist, conducted the hypnosis on the Hills and concluded that Barney's recollection was potentially a fantasy that had been inspired by Betty's dreams. Simon believed

---

[3] According to Marjorie's obituary, Marjorie had issued a statement stating that she felt, based on the latest astronomical data, that the correlation she had identified was incorrect. However, no-one can find Marjorie's statement repudiating her initial claims and its inclusion in her obituary was a surprise to many. Marjorie's niece pours doubt that Marjorie ever made such a statement.

that this was the most reasonable and consistent explanation. Barney rejected this notion, highlighting that whilst there were similarities in both of their narratives, there were portions that were unique to each of them. Barney also highlighted the physical signs such as the watches not working and a strange, discoloured spot on his car. Simon wrote about the Hill's case for the journal Psychiatric Opinion, in which he concluded that the case was a singular psychological aberration. Once the story became more widely known there were a much wider range of claims from the sceptic community as to the true origin of the Hills encounter.

In this experience we can see the regular features of future encounters such as the capture-stage, the examination, discussion of wider concepts such as origin of the occupants and the release of the abductees. Also, on completion of Simon's hypnosis sessions, all parties agree on the effectiveness of hypnosis thus cementing its use in future abduction research as the tool to unlock the memories of abductees. It is worth remembering that Dr. Simon was not a believer in UFOs or alien abduction, so claims of the therapist leading the patient are difficult to pin on Dr. Simon as much of what was uncovered had not entered the cultural mainstream for Dr. Simon to be influenced by.

The Betty Andreasson Luca Abduction

Whilst the foundations for the modern phenomena were being established, there were some outliers which, whilst were similar in appearance to experiences that had gone before, contained some elements which would prove problematic for alien abduction believers. The Betty Andreassan Luca incidents introduced some interesting elements that certainly did not fit the mould.

One January evening in 1967, Betty Andreasson was in the kitchen of her Massachusetts home with the rest of the family; seven children and her parents, all of whom were in the living room. Around 6.30pm the house was plunged into darkness for a few seconds. Suddenly, a pulsating reddish-orange light shone through the kitchen window. The children, understandably, started to panic. Betty tried to calm the children while her father looked out of the window. He witnessed a small group of short creatures who were approaching the house with a strange hopping motion. The five creatures entered the kitchen by passing through a wooden door.

As the beings entered the house, Betty's family all appeared to be frozen in time. The leader of the group was slightly taller than the others at approximately 5 feet, and this being started communicating telepathically with Betty. Each of the beings looked like the stereotypical Grey alien, and was dressed in a blue coverall type uniform, with a belt that went around the waist and across the chest and over the shoulder. Betty also claimed there was a bird-like motif on the sleeve of the uniforms.

Soon Betty reported a feeling of calmness washing over her as well as a strong sense of friendship. When Betty started to worry about the state of her family, the beings released her daughter Becky from the frozen state she had been in, to reassure Betty. Betty was then taken outside and brought onto a small craft. The craft looked like two saucers placed rim to rim. The small craft took off and docked within a larger craft. Betty then underwent the typical physical examination and then underwent a strange lesson which caused her to have a painful yet euphoric spiritual experience.

Later that night, at approximately 10.40pm, Betty was returned home by two of the original beings. The family were still in the frozen state that Betty had left them in, however, it appeared that one of the aliens had remained with the family to watch over them. Then, even more strangely, the beings put the family members to bed and left.

Shortly after the event, Betty had very limited recollection of the incident and it took sessions of regression hypnosis to unlock the full experience from her mind. As a staunch Christian, Betty did not initially think of the experience as anything UFO/ET-related. Betty believed the beings as religious or angelic in origin. In fact, further experiences unlocked through regression, detailed Betty encountering "The One", which appeared to have deeply religious overtones. Betty later went on to detail that she believed Jesus was soon to return to Earth to save us from an impending apocalypse. As the regression continued, Betty detailed encounters that stretched back as far as 1944, which puts the start of the modern abduction phenomena timeline earlier than previously believed.

The investigation into Betty's claims were very in-depth for the time: a twelve-month investigation involving several researchers from different disciplines led to a 528-page report on the incidents. Unfortunately, the investigation did not take place until ten years after the original incident. Of course, whilst there were many of the typical stages within these encounters, the heavily religious intonation of these encounters concerned many. Were the aliens really emissaries from God? Or was this a subjective interpretation based on Betty's deeply held religious beliefs?

The Allagash Waterway Abduction

The Allagash Waterway incident is an important chapter in the abduction story as it involved four experiencers. It is commonly believed, especially by sceptics, that abductions take place to individuals who could not really verify their story in any meaningful way. This incident involved four people, all initially telling the same story.

On Thursday, August 26, 1975, four friends set up their camp on Eagle Lake in Maine, with the aim to spend some time fishing. Chuck, Rak and identical twins Jim and Jack Weiner built a large bonfire to act as a guiding beacon so they could guide themselves back to their camp. The four friends launched their canoe onto the lake and after a short while noticed a large and bright sphere of coloured light hovering above the south-eastern rim of the cove. The object hovered silently around 200-300 feet in the air.

One of the group blinked the flashlight at the object and this seemed to attract the object's attention. The UFO began to move towards the canoe when suddenly a cone shaped beam of light emerged from the object and illuminated the water beneath it. Clearly concerned by this turn of events, the four fishermen began paddling for the shore to escape the object.

Due to the speed of the object the canoe was soon engulfed in the beam. However, the next thing they remembered was being in the canoe close to the shore whilst the UFO ascended into the sky and disappeared. However, all was not what it seemed. The bonfire had burnt down to embers, something that should not have happened for quite a while, indicating to the group that a period of time may have elapsed which they couldn't account for.

However strange the encounter, the men thought nothing more of it until many years later. Jim Weiner had suffered with temporolimbic epilepsy and had retold the UFO incident to his doctors, as well as other strange incidents the group had experienced. The doctor advised him to contact a UFO researcher to explore the incident further.

Professional hypnotherapist, Anthony Constantino, had agreed to hypnotise all four of the experiencers separately. Each of the four men told how they had been transported to a diffusely lit craft and underwent strange procedures conducted by the typical looking Grey alien. The men recounted that all communication was done telepathically with the aliens.

For his part, Constantino, had little experience in regressing abductees and held very little pre-conceived ideas as to the phenomena which might give the story further credibility as most sceptics will claim that hypnotherapists are very prone to leading the abductees. However, in an interview with the St John Valley Times, Charles Rak changed his story and claims he went along with the narrative for financial gain. He stands by the original UFO sighting but claims the abduction aspect of the story was fabricated. The remaining three experiencers stand by their claims and point to their hypnosis and successful polygraph tests as proof of their claims.

The Travis Walton Abduction

This high-profile case has consistently been one of the toughest for sceptics to disprove as it includes several witnesses to a UFO sighting at the start of the incident. Also, those several witnesses have continued to stick to their story despite some intense interrogation. What has also proved difficult for sceptics is the fact that Travis Walton went missing for 5 days.

The incident started on November 5, 1975, in the Apache-Sitgreaves National Forest. Travis was travelling with a logging crew, ending an exhausting day clearing the Forest as part of a government contract. As they travelled home, they witnessed a large, luminous disc shaped object hovering low above the trees. Travis was transfixed by the object and once the truck slowed, Travis jumped out and moved to get a closer look. As Travis moved closer a bluish light struck him and threw him some distance.

The sight of Travis being thrown through the air by the bluish beam panicked those remaining in the truck, causing them to flee. A short way down the road an argument had erupted between the crew and it was decided to return to see if they could help Travis. As they returned to the scene, it soon became apparent that neither the craft nor Travis were anywhere to be found. Both had vanished without a trace. After a cursory search of the immediate area, the crew decided they needed to report this to the local police.

Deputy Ellison was the first to meet with the crew and subsequently described them as very distressed by the incident. After another brief search by the officer and the crew, it was decided to leave the area and begin a more thorough search in the morning. Over the next few days, several searches were made with no joy. Aerial searches and sniffer dogs were all employed in the search for Travis. With plunging temperatures at night, the concern was that an injured and disorientated Travis would not survive for long.

Local law enforcement was keen to look for a more prosaic explanation for Travis' disappearance, including the possibility that Travis had been murdered. The remaining members of the logging crew were questioned repeatedly over the event as officers struggled to find a more earth-bound explanation for the disappearance of Travis. All members of the crew underwent a polygraph test to determine the validity of their incredible claims. Five of the crew passed the polygraph test, with the sixth member of the crew's test being deemed inconclusive.

Five days after Travis disappeared, Grant (Travis' brother-in-law) received a phone call in the early hours of the morning from someone claiming to be Travis. At first, Grant believed this might have been a joke, but felt it was worth investigating. Grant collected Travis' brother Duane, and they set off to Heber, Arizona. There they discovered a slightly confused and very disorientated Travis.

Travis explained that he had found himself on the pavement at Heber and looking up saw the mirrored underside of a rounded, silvery disk.

Travis estimated that the object was about forty foot in diameter and about fourteen feet high. Travis saw that the object was silently floating and emitting a soft warmth that he could feel on his face. The object suddenly shot up into the air emitting no sound other than the rush of displaced air. Travis walked to a nearby service station but found that it was closed, and despite knocking repeatedly, the place seemed deserted. Travis noticed a line of phone booths from where he called Grant.

On the journey back Travis was evidently disorientated, massively underestimating the amount of time he had been missing. Grant pointed out the facial hair growth Travis had and informed him of the fact he had been missing for five days.

As far as Travis was aware, his last memory of being in the woods was of him going backwards and then darkness. After that fragment of memory, Travis remembers waking on a table and briefly believing he is on a table at a hospital, although he is confused to be still wearing his work clothes. Travis starts to focus on what he believes to be doctors and nurses standing around the table. But as he focuses, he is horrified to be surrounded by three strange creatures. Travis pushes one of the creatures away and drags himself to his feet. Terrified, Travis grabs the nearest object (an unidentifiable tube) and warns the creatures to stay back.

The creatures, just under five feet tall, appear thin and weak with soft looking skin. As with many of these encounters, the creature's heads were overly large for the bodies and had extremely prominent brown eyes, which for some reason Travis found upsetting. Travis described the eyes as being twice the size of a typical human eye, with very little white showing and due to the fact that the pupils were partly hidden by the eyelids, almost appeared cat-like. Travis, expecting to have to fight the creatures, was surprised when they backed away and left him alone in the room.

During his experience, Travis encounters not only human looking beings who appear to be working with the aliens, but Travis appears to be on a Mothership due to him witnessing several small craft aboard a much larger craft.

The Travis Walton case is difficult to disprove due to the number of witnesses alone. However, it isn't the only case that features many witnesses and high strangeness.

The Linda Cortile Abduction

The Linda Cortile abduction is one of the most controversial, extremely compelling, and according to many alleged abductees, a very authentic sounding case. The many sceptics of the case highlight it is just too good to be true. The incident started on November 30, 1989, when Cortile (real name Linda Napolitano) claimed that she was abducted from her Manhattan apartment in the early hours of the morning. Linda explained that three grey-type aliens floated her out through her bedroom window and up towards a UFO that was hovering above the building. Whilst Linda's case follows many aspects of the typical abduction experience, the fact that it was alleged to have been witnessed by several people, including two security personnel (who later claimed to work for the CIA) and the then Secretary General of the United Nations, Javier Perez de Cuellar, elevates the status of this incident at the time. It is even hinted that the abduction was staged as a show of strength by the aliens. Several other witnesses would also come forward to lend credence to the fact that something strange had occurred over New York that night.

Linda could only recall segments of the experience and used hypnosis, courtesy of researcher Budd Hopkins, to recover the rest of the memories. The case is one of the most controversial due to the alleged witnessing of an actual abduction event, the calibre of the witnesses involved and the strange weirdness of the entire story. At one point, Linda is abducted by the CIA personnel who seem to think she is connected with the aliens in some way. Budd Hopkins even receives communication from the CIA personnel which either adds to the veracity of the story or is part of a cleverly constructed hoax. At times the whole incident does seem to be too good to be true in regard to the multiple witnesses.

Hopkins book *"Witnessed: True Story of the Brooklyn Bridge Abduction"* seems at times a hugely strange tale, but many abductees indicate that the post-abduction weirdness is highly representative of their own experiences.

I have highlighted these cases (and there are so many others equally as strange), as while sometimes they are very typical of the abductee experience, each one adds something to the narrative of the phenomena. Some of these aspects, such as high-level witnesses or multiple experiencers, serve to make the experience more authentic as these aspects are difficult for sceptics to explain away. How can four individuals all suffer sleep paralysis (which would be the sceptical explanation for their experience) on the same night and remember identical accounts? How could Travis Walton disappear without a trace for five days? If true, what are the implications of the witnessing of an abduction by a then high-ranking member of the United Nations and his two-man security detail.

Of course, alien abduction is not a phenomenon solely rooted in the United States, although the slightly US-centric nature of alien abduction and UFOlogy in general might give people that impression. The United Kingdom has had a curious and sometimes stranger history of alien abduction.

2 A VERY BRITISH ABDUCTION

Despite there being a dearth of books focussing on the UK abduction phenomena in comparison to the US, there have been many incidents reported in the UK which bring something to our understanding of the phenomena. There are some very interesting abduction cases in the UK, many of these seem to also hold some differences to the typical US-based experiences. As we shall see in the next few cases, the UK has hosted some equally bizarre abduction experiences.

Alan Godfrey

One of the most commonly known abduction cases in the UK and often erroneously called Britain's first abduction case by the media, is the case of Alan Godfrey. The incident occurred around 5am on 29th November 1980. Alan was investigating reports of cattle loose on a housing estate. Despite many attempts to find the cattle, Alan was coming to the end of his shift and decided to give it one last attempt before ending his shift at 6am. Alan drove up Burnley Road and after a short distance became aware of a bright light ahead of him. Alan continued driving forward until he was around 100 feet from the light. Alan saw that the light was in fact a large, fluorescent object. There were a series of windows on the upper part of the craft. The lower part of the object was rotating anti-clockwise, and this motion was making the bushes and shrubs shake. Alan decided to contact the police station for assistance but neither of his radios would work.

Suddenly Godfrey found himself 300 yards further down the road and the UFO was nowhere to be seen. Godfrey returned to the police station, and he took a colleague back to the spot where he saw the object and they both agreed that there was nothing he could have mistaken for the object. They also noticed that the spot where the object had been hovering was dry whereas the rest of the road was wet from the rain during the night. Later that day he had a flashback where he recalled, just before the object disappeared, hearing a voice say "You should not be seeing this. This is not for your eyes".

The following night Godfrey learnt that he wasn't the only witness to something strange that night. Three other police officers reported seeing a similar object some twenty minutes before Godfrey's sighting. A special constable and an anonymous caller also reported seeing a UFO close to the time that Alan saw the craft. These other witnesses gave Godfrey confidence that he had indeed witnessed something very unusual. He had also become aware of an injury to his left foot and had noticed that his new boots were damaged, as if they had been dragged over a hard surface. Godfrey had no explanation for this. After several months of unanswered questions, Godfrey decided to use hypnosis to uncover what had happened that night.

Under hypnosis, Godfrey recounts being carried and finding himself in a room. There was a table in the room and there was a bearded man wearing what appeared to be a white sheet and a skull cap. Godfrey felt he knew this person as 'Joseph'. Godfrey also noticed eight smaller, metallic figures in the room as well. In the corner Godfrey also noticed a large black dog. Godfrey was helped onto the table where he started to feel intense pain in his head, which Joseph eased. The metallic creatures removed his left boot and examined his foot. Some bracelets were put onto his right wrist and left ankle, with the bracelets then being plugged into a machine. As Godfrey led there, a series of images from his earlier life flashed into his mind and he got the impression that he had met Joseph before and saw an image of a large ball of light hovering in his childhood bedroom.

After the hypnosis session both Godfrey and the hypnotherapist (Dr. Joseph Jaffe) were at a loss to explain the content of the sessions. I find it quite interesting that Alan was carried onto the craft despite many later accounts feature abductees being floated into craft. Also, aside from a large black dog being present, one strange feature which is quite often noticed in many early UK abductions is the prevalence of robotic type beings.

Robert Taylor
When Robert Taylor came home from work his wife was shocked to discover he was dishevelled, muddy and his clothing had been torn. Sensing something terrible had happened she called the police and their doctor. The doctor soon arrived and treated Robert for grazes to the chin and thigh. Robert explained to the police that he had parked his pickup truck on the side of a road close to the M8 motorway and along with his dog, walked along the forest path up to Dechmont Law. According to Robert, he came across a "flying dome" hovering above the ground in a forest clearing. Robert described the object as being made from a dark metallic material, which had a rough texture similar to sandpaper. There was an outer rim on the object which had a set of small propellers.

Robert claimed that the air was thick with a foul smell, similar to "burning brakes". Smaller spheres, which he explained looked like sea mines, had grabbed him and were dragging him back to the larger object. Robert lost consciousness but eventually awoke to find that the object was gone. Robert's dog was uncontrollable and was panicking. Robert was unable to calm the dog as he had discovered that he had now somehow lost his voice. Robert also noted that his trousers had been torn. Robert left the scene and returned to his truck, but he was unable to start it and had to walk home.

The police accompanied Robert to the site where the incident took place and discovered ladder shaped indentations in the ground where the larger object had been and other ground indentations that Robert claimed were made by the smaller spherical mine-like objects. The police took Robert's claim seriously and logged the incident as a criminal assault. Despite a detailed police enquiry, the police were left baffled. Whilst this was no typical abduction and no beings were seen, there was obviously an attempt by something to drag Robert back to the larger object.

Garry Wood and Colin Wright
On 17th August 1992, Ambulance technician Garry Wood and his friend Colin Wright were travelling south of Glasgow on the A70

when they noticed a large, black object in the distance. It was around 10pm and the road was quiet. The pair estimated that the object was about 20 feet high, and 30 feet wide. The object then started to move towards the travelling van and was soon hovering over the road a short distance ahead of them.

Suddenly the black object dropped a wall of light in front of the van. Both Garry and Colin blacked out and initially remember very little after that moment. The pair awoke to find that a whole hour had passed by which they couldn't account for. Also, their van was now facing the opposite direction to which they were originally travelling in, but neither of them could explain when or how they had turned around, or the fact the van was now stationary. The pair were very shaken by their experience and agreed to undergo hypnosis in an attempt to understand what happened during that missing hour.

During the hypnotic sessions, both Garry and Colin recall passing into the light and experiencing intense pain as they did so. Both men recalled being taken onto the craft by three beings. Once on the craft, the three beings removed the pair's clothing. Whilst they were onboard, Garry recalls hearing human sounding screams from a nearby room on the ship.

The pair described being examined and during that examination a taller being was present, overseeing the proceedings. This being was approximately six feet tall, a large head, dark eyes and four fingers on each hand. The tall being seemed to do all the communicating via telepathy.

Colin remembers being placed in a transparent container and was able to also see that there were other men and women held in similar containers. Colin also remembered seeing a device rising from the floor. The device was long and thin, with two glowing red lights set into one of the sides. The device moved up and down, left to right, continuously. Colin felt that this device was somehow scanning him.

Garry remembers being led on a flat table, unable to move but not restrained by any means that he could see. In the centre of the room was a black, lens shaped device, which reminded Gary of a Mobius strip, the way that it twisted in on itself. Its function wasn't clear to

Garry but he noted that it made a whooshing noise as if air was being displaced. In his subsequent hypnotic sessions, Garry remembers seeing 20 to 30 creatures all present in the room, including a smartly dressed human. Garry was able to communicate telepathically with the tall being and he asked why they were doing this. "Sanctuary" came the strange response. The tall being continued, "We are here, and we are coming here". In other conversations, the tall being stated that "In many ways you are more advanced than us, but you have been 'capped'. Our existence is much like your own, we also have concerns and needs." What the being meant by 'capped' is unclear and open for interpretation.

In 2012 the MoD released a number of files including a two paged report entitled "Unexplained Aerial Sightings", which documented some of the aspects of the case and included six other alien encounters in Scotland.

Beings from Janos
What I find quite interesting when looking at UK-based abduction incidents, is that a lot of the earlier abduction incidents in the 1960-70s feature many aspects of the abduction phenomena but rarely do we see the archetypal Greys in these incidents. The Greys have become the stereotypical image of the alien abductor, but in many early UK incidents they are rarely seen. The following incident illustrates this perfectly.

The Mann family: John and his wife Gloria, their three-year-old daughter, and John's sister, Frances, were travelling back to their home in Gloucester. They were travelling along the A417 when they noticed a bright light in the sky, which appeared to be keeping pace with them. John pulled over by a hedge but when he got out of the car the light had disappeared. Suddenly, a large UFO appeared in front of the car and after a short while the object started to drift off to the right, behind some trees. They also noted a strange swooshing sound that seemed to accompany the craft. The family became scared and decided to drive off.

Their journey then started to take a surreal turn. Despite not having any possibility to turn off the road, the road seemed unfamiliar, there were tall hedges where there shouldn't be, the road became quite winding when they knew it should be quite straight. The journey seemed to be taking far longer than it should have, and all the time the UFO was still tracking them. When they reached their destination, they noted that it was an hour later than they would have expected. John was quite concerned and rang the RAF to enquire if any experimental aircraft had been tested in the area, but the RAF couldn't shed any light on what they had seen.

Frances left to travel to her home and John and Gloria went to bed feeling decidedly unwell. After about an hour's sleep they both awoke to hear the same swooshing sound they had heard when they saw the UFO. The sound soon subsided, and they returned to sleep. However, for the next few days they noticed strange bruises on their body and parts of their skin were decidedly itchy.

Around seven days after the incident John was suffering with the flu and went to bed. John dreamt that he and his family all got out of the car and entered the object via a doorway to the side of the object. Once inside they followed a corridor and came across several doorways. John entered one doorway whilst the others entered another doorway. The room John had entered had an array of electronic looking equipment on the walls and a large black chair in the centre of the room. John received telepathic instructions to sit in the chair, which he duly did. Once in the chair restraints pinned his legs into place and a pencil thin beam of light came from a panel in front of him and appeared to scan his entire body. Once the scan was complete, the restraints retracted, and he got out of the chair. John walked back to the corridor and was joined by the others. They all walked down the corridor and back to the car.

Several days later, Frances also had a dream which featured a similar story to John's. Natasha was also having dreams where she was being examined by aliens in silver jump-suits. Natasha also started to have recollections during waking hours. She also remembered being given a 'fizzy drink' which was designed to help them forget about the experience. It became evident to all the experiencers that something had occurred to them that night and they agreed to undergo hypnotic regression.

Between John, Frances and Natasha, the following story was established. Soon after witnessing the UFO, the car came to a stop and was soon surrounded by a dense fog or mist. The craft was now hovering over the road. Several shadowy figures began to emerge from the mist. Dressed in silver jumpsuits they surrounded the car. The family got out of the car and were enveloped in a beam of white light. One of the aliens turned off the lights on the car and turned off the ignition. The family then remembers being floated into the craft, finding themselves in a large circular room. The family were then put on to a moving ramp which took them up to a balcony section where there were several silver-suited aliens waiting for them. One of the aliens welcomed them and explained that they would be medically examined to see how similar they were to the aliens. The alien went on to explain that once this was done then they would be happy to answer questions from the family. The alien then stated that the family would be shown around the craft and then returned to their car as if nothing had happened.

The children remained with the mother as all the other adults were led to separate rooms. Similar to John's dream, Frances found herself in a room with a similar examination chair. Frances got onto the chair after receiving a telepathic message to do so. She found herself pressed into the chair as if a heavy weight was upon her and a dazzling light was then shone into her eyes. She became aware of two silver-suited men that were now in the room. They seemed to be attending to the control panels on the wall. Frances recounted that they were around 6ft tall, with blonde cropped hair.

After being in the chair for around 20 minutes, Frances was able to get up from the chair. She was told that there wasn't much difference between humans and the aliens, and that any differences would probably adjust themselves over time. Frances was then taken to what she described as a café type area, where several aliens were relaxing and drinking. She was approached by an alien who identified himself as the pilot of the craft. He explained that they had left their home planet Janos, around two Earth years ago. He went on to explain, with the use of images and film, how they had to leave their planet due to a terrible accident. Frances was shown a film of people dying of radiation sickness on Janos, whilst he explained how their planet had been destroyed. He then showed still images of how the planet used to be. Suddenly he explained that she had to go and led her through the corridors to reunite her with Gloria and the children.

John had been led to the examination room by someone he assumed was the captain of the craft. Once in the room, two females joined them, and they explained that the examination was necessary as they were planning to settle upon Earth. John was then strapped to the chair and several psychological tests were performed on him. Whilst in the chair, John felt a movement that he felt was the craft taking off. Once the examination was over, the two females informed John that they had taken blood samples. John was given a tour of the ship, at one point passing a porthole, through which John could only see darkness, further confirming John's suspicions that the craft had indeed taken off.

John asked the captain where they had come from and with the help of images on a screen, John was shown the journey in reverse until they arrived at Janos. The film continued to show how beautiful the planet had once been.

John was reunited with the rest of the family and was told that they would now be returned. They were told that they would meet again and that they would recognize them. The family were offered a drink which, they were informed, would help them forget their experience. They were led back to their car, which was already deposited back on Earth, and watched the craft ascend and disappear.

What is interesting about this case to me is the inclusion of apocalyptic imagery, which became a common theme in many subsequent abduction cases.

Carol and Helen Thomas
Mother and daughter Carol and Helen Thomas were walking the short journey to their place of work, when they became aware of a humming sound coming from above. As they looked up to see where the noise was coming from, they saw a bright searchlight beaming down on them, and the light seemed to be getting bigger and bigger as if it were descending towards them. Suddenly they found themselves stumbling down the alley to get to work, but when they arrived, they noticed that they were very late for work. In fact, they were several hours late. They were also confused as to why they were now soaking wet, yet judging by the dry ground, there had not been any rain.

Soon after this incident both women reported sunburn type blisters on their arms and faces, as well as nosebleeds and discharges from their navels. Extremely confused by the incident and its aftermath, both women underwent hypnosis to try to discover what had happened to them.

Whilst under hypnosis, Carol remembered the light that had been above them was now somehow under them. Carol recalls being able to see the Moon and was travelling towards it. She then suddenly found herself in a white room which had windows all around it. Carol remembers being naked and strapped to a table, with a wet cloth draped over her legs. Carol remembers being surrounded by typical greys but there was a tall blonde, human looking entity who was wearing a silver suit with a badge on it. The aliens inserted a glass tube through her navel, which she believes was used to remove eggs from her ovaries. A large cap-like device was placed on her head and Carol was then able to see images such as a collection of shapes and then a war film. After that ended Carol found herself back in the alley.

Helen also found herself strapped to a table, next to her mother. Helen was also naked with a similar wet cloth draped over her legs. Helen believed that there was a small camera hovering over her during the examination. The aliens had a small silver rod, with what appeared to be a small silver ball on the end. The silver rod was pushed up into her nose, and when the rod was removed the silver ball had gone. Also, a thin wire was fed into Helen's ear, whilst a glass tube was inserted into her navel. Helen also believes that two wires were also inserted into her cervix. Helen also claimed that something was removed from her.

Helen also had a cap-like device placed on her head and then was shown a series of images, similar to her Mother. Helen reported seeing her mother with a tall female alien who was also wearing a silver suit. Helen said that the alien looked like a beautiful woman, very human-like in appearance. Both women reported that the alien's touch seemed damp. Helen also recalled previous abduction incidents from her childhood. One memory involved her being taken as a young child and examined whilst being watched by what she described as "weird-looking children". Helen then became aware of being back in the alleyway with her mother.

Ilkley Moor

On the December 1st, 1987, Philip Spencer was walking across Ilkley Moor to visit his father. As he crossed the moor, he became aware of a low, humming sound. Suspecting it was an aircraft, Philip continued his journey, but he soon noticed a small green/grey creature approaching him. The creature scurried away but Philip shouted towards it forcing the creature to turn. As the creature turned, Philip took a photograph which has gone on to become one of the most debated photographs in UFOlogy. Philip also noticed on a rocky outcrop there was a large UFO, which was the source of the humming. Without warning, the UFO shot up into the air.

Philip decided to go back to Ilkley but as he arrived, he noticed that he had a large chunk of missing time. Concerned by the missing time and the encounter on the Moor, Philip travelled to nearby Keighley to get his pictures developed as there was a 1-hour photo development shop.

Once Philip got the pictures back, he discovered that one image contained what looked like a short, grey/green creature with short legs and long, thin arms. Philip approached a local UFO group as he wanted to discover more about the missing time aspect of the incident. Under hypnosis he revealed that when he first encountered the creature, he had become paralysed. Philip then felt himself being levitated over to the waiting craft.

Philip became aware of being in an extremely brightly lit room, led on a table. Philip remembered being told not to be afraid. A beam of light passed over Philip. Philip closed his eyes and felt something uncomfortable going into his nose. Philip was then given a brief tour of the craft, even seeing the Earth through a porthole window. Philip then saw some films showing apocalyptic scenes.

Philip then remembers being left by the alien in the same location from which he was taken. Philip recalled seeing the creature walk away from him back towards the craft. Philip called out after the alien and took the now infamous photograph.

Joyce Bowles

In November 1976, Joyce Bowles was giving her neighbour, Ted Pratt, a lift from Winchester to Chilcomb. On their journey the car suddenly began to shake and shudder in a violent fashion and then shuddered to a standstill. Both Joy and her passenger became aware of a shrill noise similar to a kettle whistling. They both then noticed a 15-foot-long glowing cigar shaped object hovering over the deserted road. There were three figures watching Joyce and Pat through windows in the object. Suddenly a figure appeared next to Joyce's car. The figure was around 6ft tall, long blonde hair and was wearing a silvery boiler suit. Joyce described his eyes as pink and very bright. Joyce found his gaze horrible, but Ted felt only peace and tranquillity when the figure looked at him. After looking at Joyce and Ted, the creature looked at the car's controls and then wandered to the back of the car. Both the figure and the cigar shaped object suddenly disappeared. That same weekend there were eight separate sightings of a glowing cigar shaped object and one report of a tall figure in a silver boiler suit in the same area.

Six weeks after this incident Joyce and Ted were driving along the same route when they noticed a strange orange glow in the sky. They suddenly found themselves in a strange room with three tall humanoids. All three humanoids were wearing silver jumpsuits, tall, pointed jackboots and a belt with a glittery stone in the middle. The three humanoids were talking in a strange language but seemed to repeat the word "mi-ee-ga" frequently.

Ted was asked by the humanoids to walk up and down and to tell them if he felt hot or cold. Both Joyce and Ted were then shown a series of transparent images that were incomprehensible to them. The entities explained that "This is our field". Ted, a farm manager, asked them if they were talking about pasture, which seemed to annoy the entities. The entities then assured Joyce and Ted that they had not come to invade. Joyce retorted by saying that Hitler had said something similar. Suddenly there was a flash of light and they found themselves back in the car but parked by a river on a road they were not familiar with.

March 7th, 1977, Joyce was driving down a country lane with her friend Ann Strickland when the car suddenly lost power and slowed to a standstill. Both Joyce and her friend got out of the car and noticed a glowing oval shaped object which was making a low humming sound. Both Joyce and Ann reported seeing a man get out of the object and walk towards Joyce with his hands held open towards her. The man took Joyce's hands and looked her up and down. Both women reported being terrified. The man started to speak to them in a strange language, but suddenly switched to speaking broken English. Joyce explained that the man told her something that she could never repeat.

After delivering his message, the man turned and walked to the object. Joyce and Ann both witnessed the object rise into the air and disappear from view. Ann explained that she did not hear what message was imparted to Joyce and explained that Joyce refused to tell her.

In June, 1977, Joyce had her final encounter, again with Ted as the passenger. Her car came to a gentle stop when they encountered two long haired entities. Wearing dull metallic suits, the entities explained that they were trying to help mankind avoid war. The entities explained that mankind would destroy themselves as well as pollute the atmosphere. The entities said their goodbyes and retreated to their craft, which launched into the sky and disappeared.

Joyce took the secret message from the aliens to her grave in 2010.

Gabriella Versacci

Gabriella Versacci (pseudonym) was travelling to visit a sick friend from her home in Taunton to Wellington late at night on October 16, 1973, when she noticed a single bright light hanging stationary on the dark B-road ahead. Gabriella knew the roads well enough to know that there should not be a light at that point in the road. Suddenly her car lost power and she found the car gently slowing before coming to a full stop. With the car stopped at the side of the road, Gabriella was confronted with the darkness.

She decided to open the bonnet and see if there was anything she could do to get the car started. As she peered into the engine, she became aware of a humming noise, which was gradually building in volume and intensity. As she went to get back into the car, a heavy hand rested on her shoulder with the sensation that it was trying to push her down to the ground. As she turned to look at her attacker, she was stunned to notice that "it" was very tall, dark in colour and metallic.

Gabriella regained consciousness after briefly blacking out. Her large attacker, which she assumed was a robot of some description, was now standing in a field next to a large, very bright object. Gabriella recounted that the object was rounded at the top and flattened at the bottom. Oblong windows ran along the middle of the object which she estimated to be around 20 foot high and 40 feet across. After taking in the scene, Gabriella passed out.

Gabriella awoke to find herself strapped to a table by rubber-looking bands at her hands and feet. She could see that she was in a circular room and could also see that the robot she had encountered earlier was against the wall, looking as if it had been switched-off. Gabriella noticed how cold it was, partly because she was now naked and only covered by a blue blanket. The whole temperature of the room seemed to be very cold.

From out of view, three men came into the room. Two remained at the left of the table whilst the other went to the foot of the table and picked up some cubes. These cubes were placed onto a rail which ran the length of the table. One cube was by her head, one by her waist and one by her feet. When in position the cubes began to glow. Gabriella remembered the three men as being fair skinned, slim build and were wearing outfits similar to a surgeon, with face masks, long aprons and skull caps tied at the back. Their eyes were rounder than a humans and were devoid of emotion.

The being at the foot of the table retrieved a number of instruments that he used on Gabriella. A small knife was used to take a nail cutting. Then a blood sample was taken into a small plastic looking bottle. The examiner had a small device in the palm of his hand which he passed over her body. The device glowed with a variety of intensities, depending on the part of the body it was over. A large black rubber cup was placed over her groin. This caused a great deal of discomfort. The examiner placed a new black blanket over her entire body which she took as a sign of the examination being over. Gabriella kept looking towards the robot she had encountered earlier. The examiner noticed Gabriella repeatedly looking at the robot and he suddenly explained to her in near-perfect English that the robot was designed to collect specimens for them to study. The examiner then removed the three cubes from the rail and the three men then exited the room.

Gabriella was still stuck on the table when she noticed one of the men had returned. He lifted the blanket and emotionlessly looked at her body. The being then took what looked like a small pin and placed it on her thigh, rendering Gabriella paralysed. The being climbed onto the table and raped her. Once finished, the being placed the blanket back over Gabriella and left the room. The three men soon returned, removed the blanket and then removed the pin from her thigh. Gabriella passed out.

Gabriella woke up to find herself standing back on the road by her car, fully clothed. She jumped into the car which started immediately, showing no sign of the problems earlier. Gabriella drove home arriving at 2.30am, in a distraught state.

Jane Murphy

In 1981, Jane Murphy of Birstall, West Yorkshire, retired to bed in an exhausted state only to awake several hours later with the uneasy feeling that there was something wrong. As she lay there, she became aware that she could not hear her husband breathing. She also had an overwhelming feeling that there was something in the room. Jane suddenly found herself in a field, not that far from where her mother lived. Hovering over the field was a large UFO. Jane was panicked as she had no understanding of how she had got to the field. That panic intensified when she noticed several humanoids approaching her across the field. One of the humanoids grabbed her and held a cloth to her mouth and nose. Jane decided to feign collapse. Whether that initially fooled her captors is unclear as another humanoid gave her an injection that rendered her unconscious.

When she awoke, she found herself in a strange room, surrounded by several humanoids. The male humanoid appeared to be fairly human looking but with big black eyes. He was accompanied by a female humanoid who instructed Jane to bathe. After leaving the bathing area, Jane was directed onto a table in the middle of the room. The male entity was there alone now, and he positioned himself close to Jane, staring into her eyes. Jane explained that she felt mesmerised by the big, black eyes and soon felt that he was in some way seducing her. Afterwards Jane was unsure whether she was seduced or raped, but also confessed to having the best sex of her life. During the sex, Jane found the humanoid had a curious smell on them. Something Jane described as "inhuman". After the act, she asked the humanoid why she had been chosen. Telepathically the humanoid answered, very unemotionally, "Because we love you".

The other aliens now returned to the room and started to examine Jane. This included a gynaecological exam which was performed using a long, thin device. Once the examination was over Jane was given a tour of the ship. At the end of the tour Jane was given some pills to take, along with a drink.

Suddenly Jane was aware of her alarm clock going off and was back in her own bed. Jane felt she needed a bath and once in the bath started scrubbing to try and get the "inhuman" smell off her. She also discovered puncture marks on her neck from where the aliens had injected her. She then felt a curious sensation in her abdomen, a sensation she experienced when pregnant. Jane tried to pass this off as a crazy dream, but when her period was late, she started to panic.

Jane went to the doctor who assured her that was not pregnant but did notice that she had a vaginal infection. The doctor gave Jane some strong antibiotics to clear the infection. Hoping that this would be the end of the matter, Jane was disappointed when the aliens returned a few nights later. The aliens spent the time asking Jane questions around human reproduction. Jane soon was plagued by a dream that she had given birth to an alien child with blonde hair and big black eyes. The strain of this and her previous experiences were pushing Jane towards a breakdown, coupled with the fact that her marriage was also under strain due to the experiences. Jane soon sought help and uncovered abduction experiences from the age of 16 onwards.

*

What I find interesting in many of the abduction encounters in the UK, especially during the 1950s/60s/70s is that the stereotypical Grey alien does not feature that often. During this time, tall Nordic looking aliens, or more human looking aliens are the main abductors while the typical Grey type alien starts to become more prevalent during the 1980s onwards (although they did appear prior to the 1980s, but more sporadically).

As previously stated, there seems to be more incidents that feature robot-like entities that function as sample collectors. The incidents of people getting floated through walls and into craft again becomes more prevalent as time goes on. We also see in the early UK abduction reports incidents where the abductees are given drinks and sometimes pills to help them forget their experiences. This seems to be another trend which seems to feature regularly but seems to be missing from later abduction accounts. Another disturbing trend in many of the earlier UK-based abduction accounts are the incidents of rape or sexual assault. There are also several UK abduction encounters which seem to be instigated purely to facilitate a rape or sexual assault, with many of the usual abduction stages such as ship tour, medical examination or philosophical discussion missing from that specific abduction scenario.

However, despite the many claims of alien abduction, there is a lack of evidence other than the experiencers testimony. It is this lack of evidence that fuels the sceptics belief that these events do not happen and in fact have a more mundane origin. As with all aspects of the paranormal, nothing is ever straightforward...

3 THE SCEPTICAL VIEWPOINT

Alien abduction? It just doesn't happen.

That is the sceptical and general scientific opinion in a nutshell: It just doesn't happen. Ever since the apparent upsurge in reports of abductions in the late 1980's and early 1990's, sceptics and scientists have been of the opinion that alien abductions do not take place and are the product of, well, insert whichever of your chosen theory rings true. There are plenty of sceptical theories to choose from.

However, scientist & sceptic Susan Clancy believes she has pulled together what she claims is a unified theory of why people believe they have been abducted by aliens. Nothing in her theory is particularly new for those who have had an interest in the alien abduction phenomena. In reality, Clancy has just unified the various individual theories put forward by other sceptics and scientists such as sleep paralysis, cultural influences and psychological needs.

In her book *'Abducted: Why people believe they have been abducted by aliens'*, Clancy puts together a theory that sleep paralysis, coupled with influences from the media, also with contamination from the available UFO/ET literature, plus dubious therapists reinforcing abductees beliefs, all flavoured with a desire for belonging in this cold, empty universe, make people believe they have been abducted by aliens. Judging by Clancy's claims, there seems to be a need for a lot of separate components to be working closely together to make people believe they have been abducted by aliens.

The main issue with this attempt at a unified theory of why Clancy thinks people believe they have been abducted by aliens is that all the core components of this theory aren't as water-tight as she (and others) would have you believe. With that in mind, would all these components gel together as effectively as she would like you to believe?

Sleep Paralysis

Sleep paralysis has long been used as an explanation as to why people believe they have been abducted by aliens. What sleep paralysis is, is when some people are falling asleep or just when they are waking, they are unable to move. It is during this state that many people experience vivid hallucinations and report sensing presences in the room. The disruption of REM sleep is widely believed to be the root of the sleep paralysis experience, but it is proving difficult to empirically prove. It is worth remembering that scientists' understanding of sleep paralysis is still very limited. It was only as recently as 2012 when Toronto researchers Patricia Brooks and John Peever discovered the chemicals and nerve receptors involved in sleep disorders such as sleep paralysis. There are still many unanswered questions around sleep paralysis. According to research, 8% of the population suffer from sleep paralysis but that research concedes that there "there is no standard definition or etiology to diagnose sleep paralysis"[4].

However convenient a theory that may be for the sceptics and scientists, it isn't as straightforward as it would first appear. The odds of someone suffering from sleep paralysis *and* believes they have been abducted by aliens *and* have become well versed in the UFO/ET literature *and* have become influenced by the relevant media *and* feel lost and disconnected in this empty void of a universe, is ridiculously slim. However, this forms the basis of Clancy's theory.

There is one factor that spectacularly debunks the entire sleep paralysis theory, and that is that a fair proportion of abduction experiences do not happen in the bedroom. People are abducted from cars, people are abducted in the environment during daylight hours. There is this fallacy amongst sceptics and scientists that

---

[4] "Sleep Paralysis, a Medical Condition with a Diverse Cultural Interpretation" - https://www.ncbi.nlm.nih.gov/pmc/articles/PMC6082011/

abductions take place only in the bedroom at night. However convenient that is for their theory, it simply isn't the case. Whilst some abduction experiences do take place in the bedroom, until the theory can account for *all* instances of abduction, sleep paralysis as an explanation for alien abduction fails spectacularly.

There are other issues with the sleep paralysis theory. Namely, how can abductees all experience the same hallucination as each other? The odds that during a sleep paralysis episode, all abductees will see exactly the same scenes and experience them in exactly the same order, time and time again, are astronomical.

What would cause people to potentially see such identical images? Well, according to Clancy's unified theory, the media and its influence is the root of such identical hallucinations.

The Media Influence

It would be foolish to try and deny that the media does not influence us all on at least a superficial level. Advertisers and marketers have been utilising the power of the media to influence us to buy their products since the beginning of the mass media. However, judging by the content the media delivers, items regarding UFOs and alien abduction are very limited. Are we to assume that people who believe they have been abducted by aliens only watch films and programs about UFOs and abductions? We can't assume that without some serious research. If we were to follow this line of logic, then those people who suffer from sleep paralysis but do not watch UFO/alien abduction related programs should have sleep paralysis episodes full of soap stars, TV stars and the most famous Hollywood actors. However, this isn't the case. The theory of media influence coupled with sleep paralysis as a starting point for people's belief that they've been abducted by aliens is full of holes.

Even if we were to study the link between the media and people believing they were abducted by aliens, those films and documentaries on the subject do not go into such in-depth coverage of the subject that we find in abductees accounts. If we look at all the films that depict alien abduction, we see that either alien abduction is a small part of the overall film (such as 'Close Encounters of the Third Kind'), or the level of detail within the film is nowhere near as complex as in abductee accounts. Even if we look at the film 'Communion', based on Whitley Streiber's book of the same name, the film does not go into the granular detail that we find in abductee accounts. The same can be said for the documentaries on the subject of alien abduction: the detail contained in these documentaries is not detailed enough in comparison to abductee accounts. These programs and films deal with the broad concepts of abduction but do not go into the fine detail you get with abductees accounts. So where does that extra detail come from? Evidently, it isn't from the mass media or the media that covers the UFO/Abduction subject.

Many sceptics continue to argue that early science fiction is what influenced the modern abduction theory. But if we look at those initial broadcasts, they are nothing like the typical abduction experience as reported by the experiencers themselves. Many sceptics have argued that the first widely disseminated abduction experience, reported by Betty and Barney Hill, was influenced by an episode of 'The Outer Limits' which was broadcast a few days prior to their experience. However, while this episode (*The Bellero Shield*) features aliens, it isn't about alien abduction and doesn't feature many of the aspects that occur in the Hills and other abductees encounters. Also, much of the early science fiction featured robots, death rays, interplanetary warfare etc and such elements are rarely featured in abductees reports. If we are to follow this theory, the science-fiction film 'Avatar' has been seen by enough people to ensure that future alien abductions will be performed by blue aliens with dreadlocks. Also, one of the earliest recognised modern abduction accounts was by farmer Antonio Vilas Boas in 1957, which happened long before the rise of such widely available TV science fiction. So how was Boas influenced this early in the phenomena?

The media influence theory then focuses on the books about the subject that supposedly influence abductees. However, the vast majority of abductees claim to have no interest in UFOs, alien abductions or even science fiction prior to acknowledging their experiences. They usually begin reading about the subject *after* they start coming to terms with their experiences. So, if we're not seeing that level of detail in the TV/Film-based media, and many abductees/experiencers are not reading about the subject prior to acknowledging their experiences, where is this information coming from? If, as we suspect, there were much earlier 'paleo-abductions', how does Clancy's theory of media influence apply here?

Which neatly brings us to another branch of Clancy's unified theory of why people believe they have been abducted by aliens: the topic of "contamination".

Contamination

The term 'contamination' is used in reference to the theory that abductees may have been influenced by reading material on the subject of UFOs or alien abduction. This theory also applies to abductees who speak to other abductees and absorb their experiences or aspects of their experiences and make them their own. Again, the lack of evidence for this claim is somewhat troubling. As stated before, most abductees do not have an interest in UFOs, aliens or even science fiction prior to discovering their experiences, so they usually begin reading about such subjects after they start to come to terms with their experiences.

Most abductees read 'Communion' by Whitley Streiber, most abductees will read books by John Mack or Budd Hopkins because they are considered by many as the most informative on the subject. Proving that this has influenced their claims of alien abduction is important but is not tackled by Clancy's research. Social contagion, especially through the global population of abductees, is a fascinating prospect but again there is little research to back the idea up.

Regression

Therapists come in for some severe criticism in Clancy's unified theory. Whilst she does only write in generalised terms, she does raise some important points, but also fails to see the real issue which is that a poor therapist does not necessarily tarnish the tools he/she uses. It only shows them as a bad therapist. There are certainly some concerns we do need to address in-regards to the use of hypnosis especially in connection with abductees, and this will be covered in a subsequent chapter.

According to Clancy, people who go to therapists believing they have been abducted by aliens have their beliefs re-enforced and expanded on by sub-standard therapists. As a trained clinical hypnotherapist and psychotherapist myself, I feel there are some huge assumptions being made by Clancy (and others) with very little evidence. The fact is, that there are very few therapists (especially in the UK) who actually believe in alien abduction and certainly would not have the knowledge as to where to start in dealing with it, let alone influencing alleged abductees.

As a very brief study, I contacted 100 hypnotherapists all chosen randomly by someone else. Using a simple telephone interview, the following was ascertained:

- All 100 had very little knowledge of alien abduction.

- All 100 felt they would not be able to deal with someone claiming to have been abducted by aliens.

- None of the hypnotherapists surveyed mentioned alien abduction on their website.

- Of the 100 surveyed, 99 of the hypnotherapists surveyed did not mention regression, age regression or recovering memories on their website, social media or literature.

- Only one of the 100 surveyed listed Past Life Memories, but did not mention alien abduction, age regression or recovering memories other than Past Life Memories.

- All 100 therapists surveyed believed that regression was a suitable tool for recovering memories.

We can see that just by a very small sample of professional therapists, there is very little chance of an abductee being influenced by their therapist into thinking they have been abducted by aliens.

(During my training, the use of hypnotic regression was discussed and practised. During one of the first sessions dealing with regression, someone asked the tutor if he had anyone come to him as a client who believed they had been abducted by aliens. He thought for a moment and said "Anyone who comes to you and claims they have been abducted by aliens is mentally ill." That for me encapsulates much of the thinking on alien abduction by a large portion of therapists, especially in the UK)

It is a fair assumption that the vast majority of therapists within the United Kingdom do not believe in alien abduction. In 2001, The National Council for Hypnotherapy in the UK issued a statement on the subject of alien abduction:

> *"With the recent interest in this phenomenon, the National Council for Hypnotherapy issues the following guidelines.*
>
> *Alien Abduction Clients (AAC) are to be treated with the same respect and courtesy as any other client. Regression techniques that should be utilised with AACs should follow these guidelines:*
>
> *a. Non Directive*
>
> *b. Non Leading*
>
> *c. Preferably Indirect*
>
> *The therapist must also be aware of the implications of False Memory Syndrome (FMS). We recommend that therapists should not introduce the subject of Alien Abductions unless the client refers to it in the first instance. Additionally, therapists should not engage in corroborating these incidents. Therapists should take a neutral stance on the existence of Alien Abductions.*
>
> *Because of the necessity of regression in AACs it is essential that therapists ensure that clients' full medical and mental health history is taken before the commencement of treatment."*

This highlights the fact that a good therapist can use regression without leading the client/experiencer and they should not be referring to alien abduction unless the client does. More importantly, the statement goes on to highlight the importance of not corroborating the incidents and remaining neutral.

To make a wide sweeping claim that therapists are reinforcing the belief that patients are being abducted by aliens needs some good, solid evidence. Clancy does not provide that evidence. That is not to say there aren't bad therapists out there, there obviously are, but we will discuss some of the important issues around the use of hypnosis later, but suffice to say, again Clancy fails to provide sufficient evidence of her claims. It's all too generalised with little hard data.

However, Clancy also has seemed to forget that many abductees' memories are not reclaimed via hypnosis and are in fact conscious memories, or fragments of memories. It seems that many abductees become more aware of what is happening to them over time, and the memory blocks that some abductees seem to have gradually disappear. So, if some abductees are having conscious recall of what happened to them, then that opens a whole new vista in considering what is happening to these people.

The need for 'Connection'

The desire for connection is a curious direction for Clancy to then take in her unified theory of why people believe they were abducted by aliens. The need for connection is a fairly universal need and I wouldn't consider that something that was particularly unique to people who believed they had been abducted by aliens. In fact, people who claim to be abductees find themselves isolated further as very few people believe in the phenomena. Abductees often find themselves open to ridicule which can isolate them further, which makes Clancy's claim that alleged abductees are using such claims to achieve a greater connection, slightly spurious.

Research Techniques

In order to come to her unified theory Clancy surely must have done some serious research to come to the conclusions that she has published? Nothing is ever that straightforward. The only abductees Clancy investigated were those that responded to her advert in a newspaper. Now, the overwhelming majority of alleged abductees generally do not seek to bring attention to themselves. Many feel embarrassed by what they believe is happening to them and most are afraid of the ridicule they may receive, not just in the wider community but from friends and family also. So, the chances are that Clancy has attracted those who are looking for some attention, so they might not be the best test subjects. Also by Clancy's own admission, there wasn't a huge response to the advert. So there is a strong reality that there were nowhere near enough participants for Clancy to conduct any meaningful research. Also, those who did respond were simply interviewed. There was no meaningful investigation to the respondents claims of being abducted by aliens. Which is altogether curious as Clancy claims to be a serious scientist, but her research into this field is evidently lacking any meaningful depth.

Fantasy Proneness

One of the "symptoms' that many scientists believe they have identified as being an influencing factor on people's abduction beliefs is their propensity to fantasise. Fantasy Prone Personality (FPP) was a term coined by Sheryl C. Wilson and Theodore Barber in 1981. Wilson and Barber used the term to describe a small percentage of the population (around 4%) who were prone to fantasise a large proportion of their time. Their fantasies were so involved that those who were identified as FPP were said to be able to see, smell and touch their fantasies as if they were real, physical occurrences. This was a powerful argument levelled at abductees, because if you identified as being very imaginative as a child or identified as being able to visualise strongly, then you were labelled as fantasy prone which scientists tended to use to undermine your claims of being abducted by aliens. Because if you fantasised about other stuff, you probably fantasised about being abducted by aliens, right?

Despite heavily supposition-based research papers such as *"Fantasy Proneness, Amnesia and the UFO Abduction Phenomena"* by Susan Marie Powers MA, the link between FPP and alien abduction is tenuous at best.

False Memory Syndrome

In the 1980s, a rash of claims of Satanic abuse spread across the US. The now infamous, "Satanic Panic", saw hundreds of people claiming to have been abused by Satanic cults. Many claimants of alleged

Satanic abuse turned to hypnosis to recover memories of their abuse. Physical symptoms, physical indicators and evidence of abuse or the evidence of Satanic cults and their members was difficult or virtually impossible to find. Victims claimed to be abducted, taken to a location and often sexual encounters would take place resulting in unwanted pregnancies. Often the child would be taken from the woman and sacrificed. The parallels between the Satanic Panic and claims of alien abduction are difficult to ignore.

The use of hypnosis was widely used to recover alleged memories of Satanic Ritual Abuse (SRA) and for the most part the therapy was used to target and elicit such memories of SRA. The therapists involved claimed that the consistency of all the stories pointed to the reality of the SRA (something which abduction researchers also claim about the recovered memories of abductees). However, despite all the information gathered under hypnosis, there was never any corroborating evidence gathered to effectively prove SRA was taking place.

A survey of 2,709 American therapists found that the majority of claims of SRA came from just 16 therapists, which suggested that the determining factor in a patient making an allegation of SRA was the therapist's pre-disposition. It was also identified that therapists were found to believe patients more as the allegations of SRA became more bizarre and extreme. Again, there are parallels with the alien abduction phenomena that need to be confronted.

Whilst I do not want to gloss over some of the issues raised as fall-out of the "Satanic Panic" and their relevance to the abduction phenomenon, what about the small number of people who have conscious recollection of their abductions? How are we to blame hypnosis, sleep paralysis or false memories in these instances? What mechanism do scientists such as Clancy claim are at work here?

Whilst I have been critical of the scientific/sceptical stance, this isn't to say there aren't some major failings within the abduction community and the way it investigates the subject. Considering the issues that are about to be highlighted, it isn't surprising that there is such a sceptical backlash against the claims people make in-regards to alien abduction.

Aside from the usual sceptics there are critical claims from those who were once within the pro-ET hypothesis camp. Unfortunately, whilst the UFO community are quite vocal about their "open-mindedness", as we shall see, some of these critical claims have not provoked the appropriate response from so-called researchers, believers, and truth seekers. In fact, it seems to be extreme hostility is the first port of call from the UFO community in such instances. There are a number of valid issues these people are raising that do need addressing, however, a strong case of cognitive dissonance has occurred with many researchers and believers who seem totally sold on the idea that the theories of Hopkins, Mack and others are beyond reproach.

Leah Hayley

Leah Hayley came to prominence within the UFO/Abductee community with her 1993 book *"Lost Was The Key"*. The book detailed her account of extraordinary experiences involving non-human entities. By her own admission, "The most important thing about my case," she said, "is that my memories were of alien abductions, and that after spending thousands and thousands and thousands of dollars and years and years and years of research trying to find evidence that alien abductions occurred, the only evidence I found is of human-instigated mind control."

Leah now believes that her experiences were the result of her being an unwilling victim of mind-control experiments. Based on her study of patents and documents obtained under the Freedom of Information Act (FOIA), she believes that the alien abduction phenomena she experienced was the result of mind-control experimentation by the US government. She believes that other abductees' experiences are the result of human technology also.

Of course, it could be counter-argued that alien abductions were occurring at the same time as some government mind-control experiences. There are many theories that claim the US Government operates alongside the alien abductors. However, the claims that Hayley is now making are quite difficult for the UFO community to swallow. If Hayley's experiences were the result of mind control, then that really changes the whole picture of the alien abduction phenomena.

TESTIMONY VOLUME 1 – ALIEN ABDUCTION IN THE UK

Many fellow abductees have taken Hayley's about face as a personal insult considering she spent so much time espousing the belief in alien abduction. There have been many who have claimed that Hayley is now a paid government stooge involved in disinformation, which is sadly a fairly standard practice for the UFO community when someone says something to fundamentally undermine their own beliefs. Rather than investing the time to conduct some research into the claims, it's far easier to claim someone now works for the NSA/CIA/FBI/MI5 etc.

Of course, the evidence of Government sponsored mind control is particularly thin as a point of origin for the alien abduction phenomena. Particularly strong evidence for the existence of mind control technology is almost as rare as solid evidence of alien abduction. Despite the existence of some patents connected with the potential technology of mind control, and a long program of Government sponsored experimentation (which continues to this day), that isn't enough to label all abduction accounts as part of some mind control programme. Is that documentation that Leah Hayley has discovered enough to prove it was the reason for Hayley's apparent alien abduction? If so, does this mean that the US Government are the originators of the global abduction phenomena? The implications of that claim are staggering.

However, the existence of patents for mind control devices is misleading as just because a patent exists does not mean that the technology was successfully developed let alone whether it was actually used. In 1970, British Rail applied for a patent for a UFO-shaped nuclear powered interplanetary craft. The patent evidently existed (the patent lapsed due to renewal fees not being paid), but the craft was never workable based on the technology referenced in the patent and such technology did not exist outside of the patent paperwork. When the patent was analysed by Michael van Baal of the European Space Agency, he stated that "I have had a look at the plans, and they don't look very serious to me at all". He went on to explain that some of the technology referenced in the patent had not been invented yet[5].

---

[5] The Railway Magazine, May 1996

So, should we assume that all patents for mind control technology were ultimately successful and were deployed on un-witting citizens to create false memories of alien abduction? I think not, not without more substantial evidence. Within the field of alien abduction and all connected theories, the crucial evidence is never as strong as its proponents would have you believe.

Carol Rainey

Within the history of the alien abduction phenomena, some names have greater prominence than others, and these names are almost ubiquitous with some of the high-profile abductions cases. Budd Hopkins became one of the more readily recognisable names within the abduction phenomena and his theories still influence the direction (or lack of it – depending on your viewpoint) of the abduction phenomena. Hopkins was linked with some of the highest profile abduction cases. His books such as *"Missing Time: A Documented Study of UFO Abductions"*, *"Intruders: The Incredible Visitations at Copley Woods"* and *"Witnessed: The True Story of the Brooklyn Bridge UFO Abductions"* ensured Hopkins and the phenomena broke into the mainstream media. Along with Whitley Streiber's best-selling book *"Communion"* and John Mack's *"Abduction: Human Encounters With Aliens"*, the subject of alien abductions was now coming out of the shadows and into the limelight, and with it a whole host of people who now claimed they too had been abducted by ETs.

However, not long after Hopkins' death, his ex-wife Carol Rainey published an essay in Paratopia magazine entitled *"The Priests of High Strangeness: Co-creation of the alien abduction phenomena"*[6] which, again depending on your viewpoint, was either a huge reality check for the alien abduction phenomena or something akin to defiling the most sacred of texts.

Rainey claimed that the more sensational cases published by Hopkins (as well as those published by fellow researcher David Jacobs) such as those highlighted in *"Intruders: The Incredible Visitations at Copley Woods"* and *"Witnessed: The True Story of the Brooklyn Bridge UFO Abductions"* were not the norm for abduction experiences. Rainey also went on to say that her ex-husband was too easily influenced by the fantastical

---

[6] https://paratopia.files.wordpress.com/2013/06/paratopia-mag_vol1_1-15-11.pdf

stories some of the abductees were relating. Rainey stated that even as discrediting evidence came to light in regards to the Linda Cortile case, Hopkins continued to promote the story as it was being described to him. Rainey gave many examples of how abductees would confabulate their stories as time went on, to which Hopkins seemed ignorant.

Carol Rainey has sadly come in for huge amounts of abuse from sections of the UFO community because of her claims. Unfortunately, many missed the point that someone extremely close to some very high-profile cases was highlighting some really important issues which should be a wake-up call for all researchers and those claiming to have been abducted by aliens. Also, Rainey wasn't suddenly claiming to be a sceptic. Rainey was simply claiming that these experiences aren't quite the way researchers are presenting them. Rainey was making a fundamentally important claim that needed some serious follow-up research. What Rainey ultimately has claimed is that researchers are too influenced by their own expectations of what alien abduction experiences would be like. Rainey intimates that the realities of alien encounters may be too strange to adequately be quantified in our three-dimensional framework of existence. Now surely, that has to be listened to and studied, rather than instantly shouted down?

Maybe we've become too saddled with the beliefs and assumptions that previous researchers have rightly or wrongly made. It is easy to criticise Hopkins et al in hindsight. He was in many respects a pioneer who had nothing to benchmark himself against. But that doesn't mean that his work isn't or shouldn't be open to scrutiny. For a community that so often talks about "the truth", the UFO community seems unwilling to the point of outright hostility to consider that a re-appraisal is sometimes a good thing (especially if people close to the prevailing research are highlighting some potentially fundamental issues). This is especially important when we are dealing with some of the claims of abduction researchers and the abductees themselves.

I am not here to prove or disprove that alien abduction takes place, but I certainly feel that not everything can be taken at total face value, or that the theories of Mack, Hopkins and Jacob are beyond reproach. I have simply highlighted that we still need to remain open-minded, as the further you travel from the United States, the further the abduction phenomena deviates from the template documented by Hopkins, Mack et al.

The more we start to consider what those who were once considered credible witnesses, experiencers or researchers are saying, the more we might need to pause and consider what we actually know and how we are really quantifying what is happening to those who claim they have had an extraordinary experience. The solutions to what is actually happening to abductees will always focus on credible evidence, and to quote John Mack in his book *"Passport to the Cosmos"*, *"...marshalling evidence that might conceivably satisfy the physical sciences 'on their own turf' has proved to be an elusive task."*

4 THE PROBLEM WITH HYPNOSIS

I am in a typical hypnotherapy treatment room observing a training session with Helena, the relatively experienced hypnotherapist. Mike, her volunteer patient, is led on the couch and is going deep into a trance state. Six other trainees look on and watch the proceedings. Helena had regressed Mike to his birth. In fact, the actual moments after his delivery. Mike is sobbing almost-uncontrollable tears as he is reliving the still-born death of his twin. Mike, despite crying emotionally and describing the doctors ill-fated attempts to resuscitate his twin in great detail, is well aware in his conscious mind that there was never any twin. Helena has led her client into an emotional re-counting of the painful and tragic death of a non-existent twin.

Prior to the actual hypnotherapy session, in the client-therapist discussion that often precedes most hypnosis sessions, Mike had been complaining to Helena of something missing in his life, of never feeling completely "whole". Helena ultimately became complicit in propagating a fantasy of a non-existent twin. Mike, previously to this session, had no knowledge or belief in having a twin that died at birth.

Helena was obviously not aiming to arrive at this situation, but following on from the client's responses under hypnosis, has, unbeknown to her, helped recover/create false memories of the fictitious twin and its death. Mike has demonstrated a common attitude of patients by telling the hypnotherapist what they believe the therapist wants to hear. Some patients just want to please their therapist. It is a dynamic commonly found within many therapeutic settings. This is the power/danger of hypnosis – but is it the tool or the therapist that is to blame? Or both?

(Many abduction researchers point to the emotional responses of their client as evidence of the reality of their experiences. However, as illustrated in the session above, real tears and snot are quite easy to discover in many therapy rooms and should not be used as a guarantee of authenticity of experience).

One of the major issues with hypnosis is that we really do not fully understand how it works. The media and literature are full of miracle stories of how medical conditions were cured with the use of hypnosis. Hypnosis is often defined as a state of mental relaxation and Hypnotherapists will often use phrases such as "trance state" to describe the state the patient gets in so the therapy can work. There will be those that claims the trance state enables the therapist to communicate with the patient's subconscious mind, with the conscious mind taking a back seat, and at the subconscious level the therapist can change the behaviours of the patient for situations such as smoking cessation or weight loss, or for accessing memories. People who subscribe to the trance state theories would be known as state theorists. The sceptics will claim that what is being witnessed with hypnosis is merely role play, suggestibility, or a placebo effect. (As a result, sceptics of the trance state and its perceived working are known as nonstate theorists). To add to the general confusion around hypnosis, for every positive study on the benefits of hypnosis there will be at least one claiming its ineffectiveness.

That is not to say that hypnosis can't be very effective with certain conditions, it evidently can, but when we apply hypnosis to age regression and recovering memories, it might not necessarily be the magic key to re-discovering lost or hidden memories.

The Satanic Panic

In the United States, and to a lesser extent in the UK, the 1980s and 1990s saw a huge rise in the claims that people were being abducted and abused by a nationwide network of Satanists. There are many good books documenting the saga, but what connects alien abduction to this subject is the reliance on hypnosis to provide evidence of the satanic abuse. (There are a lot of other parallels, but that is for another time).

In the 1990s, the United States was in the throes of a moral panic led by factions of the evangelical church, which centred around the belief that Satanists were everywhere preying on the youth of America. A number of self-proclaimed experts fuelled this theory with their research. In 1990 a psychologist called D. Corydon Hammond propagated a complex theory of global ritual abuse which he claims to have evidenced purely from hypnotherapy sessions with patients[7].

Hammond claimed that there were cells of Satanists who used mind control, torture and satanic ritual abuse which created alternate personalities in his patients. These alternate personalities could be activated using code words, much like a Manchurian Candidate. Hammond claimed the victims of abuse were drawn into a dark world where they were trained as drug traffickers, child sex workers, child pornographers, prostitutes and even assassins. This cult was organised by the great and good of society, who ensured the memories of the victims were tampered with to ensure its clandestine operations could continue undiscovered. The only evidence of this conspiracy was from his patients, and the patients of other therapists who shared similar beliefs. No other evidence was ever forthcoming other than the testimony of patients.

The Paul Ingram Case

The Paul Ingram case is a particularly powerful case to consider the use of hypnosis or visualisation techniques. After Paul Ingram's daughters attended a Pentecostal retreat, they made claims that their father had sexually molested them. The daughters did not initially report the abuse after the abuse allegedly happened. The daughters reported the abuse after attending a Pentecostal retreat. The daughters were told at the retreat, by a woman who others at the retreat claimed had prophetic powers, that their father had sexually abused them. Ingram was a serving police officer at the time and was

---

[7] Hammond claimed to have received death threats after making his claims and refused to speak of the issue again. A transcript of Hammond lecturing on the subject can be found here https://newslog.cyberjournal.org/corydon-hammond-cults-ritual-abuse-and-mind-control/

first made aware of his daughter's claims when his fellow officers began formally questioning him on the allegations of abuse.

Ingram denied molesting his daughters, but he also believed they would not lie about such a matter and believed that he may have been repressing his memories of the molestation. One of Ingram's daughters then claimed two other individuals had also been involved in the molestation. Pentecostal assistant pastor John Bratun, who had also been involved in the Pentecostal retreat, began to use visualisation techniques with Ingram to help him remember the abuse.

Through this visualisation technique, Ingram "remembered" seeing the other two accused individuals in a setting where everyone was dressed in robes, all gathered around a central fire where a black cat was sacrificed. At no point in their claims of molestation had either of the daughters mentioned anything around satanic abuse, rituals, or people in robes. Ingram's son was soon brought in for questioning. Ingram's son claimed that he had been bound and gagged by a witch and forced to perform fellatio. Ingram's wife was then accused of sexual abuse by the daughters. Ingram's daughters now recalled witnessing satanic rituals, animal and infant sacrifice, being tortured and one daughter claimed that Ingram forced her to have sex with goats and dogs and photographed the intercourse.

The local Police department were becoming so concerned with the escalating claims being made by the daughters that they brought in an outside consultant, Dr. Richard Ofshe. Ingram had been using the visualisation technique suggested by Pastor Bratun under the belief that this technique would bring only true memories (because that is what Pastor Bratun had told him would happen). Dr. Ofshe tested Ingram by making a new accusation against him; that Ingram had forced his daughter to have sex with one of his sons. The daughter rejected the accusation and firmly denied it took place. Ingram claimed to have vague memories of the incident. Ingram went away and used the visualisation technique, and at a second meeting with Ofshe, Ingram claimed he had clearer memories of the event. At a third meeting, Ingram made a full and complete confession to Ofshe's fictionally based accusation.

Ingram continued to use this visualisation technique with Pastor Bratun which resulted in Ingram claiming that ten former and present employees of the Sheriff's office were involved in the satanic abuse cult. Ingram's daughter went on to claim that 20 Satanists controlled the county government, and they used their position and power to cover up the abuse.

In the run up to his trial Ingram started to have doubts about his memories and attempted to change his plea. The prosecution had dropped the satanic aspects of the case and Ingram was given a 20 year jail sentence for six counts of third-degree rape.

Ofshe believed that Ingram had been inadvertently hypnotised by authority figures that Ingram was prepared to trust and that the memories were nothing more than false memories that had been implanted through suggestion. At no time was a trained mental health professional present during these visualisation sessions. Despite the daughters providing maps to where the abuse allegedly happened, despite Ingram's property being excavated for evidence of ritual abuse and despite Sheriff Gary Edwards admitting there was no physical evidence in this case, Ingram was convicted purely on the testimony from his recovered memories. Ingram was released in 2003 after serving his sentence.

This is the real danger of false memories. This is the real danger of untrained practitioners.

Memory Wars

The accusations of Satanic Ritual Abuse during the 1980s and 90s occurred during a time where there was much discourse on the accuracy of the memories of alleged childhood abuse. Again, there are parallels to similar discussions around the recovered memories of alleged alien abduction. Several seminal books such as *"The Courage to Heal"* and the later discredited satanic abuse autobiography *"Michelle Remembers"* helped fuel the moral panic, and ultimately created the template for satanic ritual abuse claims.

In reality, the human memory is much more fallible and easier to manipulate than most people imagine. Our memory stores information in a very fragmented fashion and not in the linear fashion that we often hear therapists claim. It is not as simple as rewinding the mental recording to a specific date and time in the past. American cognitive psychologist Elizabeth F. Lotus has conducted groundbreaking work on the misinformation effect and eyewitness memory as well as research on false memories.

Loftus started to ponder on whether many recovered memories were actually false memories, created by a therapist's use of suggestive techniques. Loftus' student, Jim Coan developed a technique known as "Lost in the Mall", which was a device to see if a false memory could be produced in a series of willing test subjects. In the initial study, 25% of test subjects developed a "rich false memory" of an event that had never taken place. In further variations of the Lost in the Mall technique, it was found that on average a third of study participants could become convinced that they had gone through experiences that were highly traumatic and often impossible.

But what does that really prove to us? Some humans are suggestible, some humans are prone to confabulation and some humans want to please their therapist and will tell them what they think the therapist wants to hear. It also suggests to us that human memory has many pitfalls[8]. It ultimately points to the requirement of having a well-defined therapeutic framework for working with people who make claims such as experiencing alien abduction. This framework needs to primarily help the experiencer/patient and not purely as a resource for raw data.

Alien Abduction

Within abduction literature the assumption is that the memories of the abduction experience are either repressed as part of a self-defence mechanism protecting the brain from traumatic events, or that the abductors have either buried the memories to avoid detection or have set up some "screen-memory" to divert the attention of the abductee. Or potentially a combination of all three. Some abductees have even mentioned that during their experiences they are told they will forget or must forget what has happened to them. However, the theory of the repression of traumatic/painful memories is not agreed on by everyone. Repression of traumatic or painful memories was originally suggested by Freud but many sceptics of the concept believe that not

---

[8] "The Memory Illusion" by Dr. Julia Shaw is a great starting point on the subject.

only is repression a rare event but that current research indicates that trauma tends to heighten the memory of that event rather than repress it.

Just to further complicate the issue of memory, it seems that some abductee's memories seem to be triggered by events loosely associated with the original abduction event. It almost seems that those memories were not part of the abductees consciousness until they are triggered by some event, which seems to open the floodgates to the memories of previous experiences. These events could be experiences where they are confronted by animals such as owls or encounter strange people who do not seem "quite right".

Therapists harbour the idea that hypnosis, and particularly hypnotic regression, allows the therapist to transport the patient/abductee back to individual events and explore them further by recovering the missing pieces of the puzzle. The attitude of most hypnotherapists is that the memory is almost like a videotape that can be rewound or fast-forwarded to any event in that person's life, which allows them to document the scene presented by the patient/abductee.

Retrieving memories in this fashion obviously raises the question about the accuracy of the recovered memories. Ultimately this all tends to be based around whether memories have a meaningful or emotionally powerful component or aspect. Memories that are particularly traumatic or emotionally charged appear to be more likely to be recovered/accessed rather than a non-eventful trip to the supermarket on a wet Wednesday afternoon in November, three years ago, in which nothing of note happened. However, as we saw with the incident at the start of the chapter, strong emotions or physiological responses cannot always be used as a guide to accuracy or reality.

Ultimately, we can only gauge the accuracy of such recall by some form of independent verification, which within the realm of alien abduction becomes problematic. However, it is worth remembering that failure to accurately recover memories through hypnosis only points to a failure of memory rather than the failure of hypnosis.

Sceptics have been fond of the idea that recovered memories of alien abduction are caused by unscrupulous therapists who have planted false memories into the minds of their patients. But this is generally far from the truth. Most hypnotherapists see themselves as legitimate therapists trying to ease the problems of their patients. As we saw in Chapter 3, in a random sample of 100 therapists, not one therapist was interested in alien abduction or had dealt with patients claiming to have been abducted by aliens. This obviously leads to questions about how they would deal with a patient claiming to be abducted by aliens, but there is no reason to imagine that these therapists will start to plant false memories of what may or may not have happened, or what they believe should have happened.

Of course, some people who claim to have been abducted by aliens have approached UFO groups seeking some guidance on their experiences and have been directed to someone who can perform hypnosis but might not have had enough training in dealing with patients or views their hypnotic abilities as a route to gaining more information on the abduction subject. However, this again points to an issue with the practitioner and the application of the technique rather than the technique itself.

Sceptics will claim that abductees are easily led by their therapist, and whilst in our example at the start of the chapter this is demonstrated as very easy to achieve, but in a lot of the published literature abductees have resisted being led into false leads. This highlights a good therapeutic approach by the practitioner. For the original alien abduction therapists, such as Dr. Benjamin Simon who regressed Betty and Barney Hill, there was no preconceived alien abduction dialogue for him to draw on, so as a confirmed sceptic himself how could Dr. Simon really lead Betty and Barney? The Villa-Boas case was recounted without the use of hypnosis so where was this information coming from? It either points to a hoax or it happened. A hoax has never been proven, so that potentially leaves one option.

It is frighteningly easy to find a weekend course that will claim to be able to train you to become a "certified" hypnotherapist. As the hypnotherapy industry battles for some form of credibility, these weekend courses point to the problem with hypnosis, inasmuch as it is an easy skill to learn initially but there needs to be a lot more training to learn how to deal with the complex psychological and emotional needs of patients. This is especially true when confronted with people who claim to have been abducted by aliens.

However, therapists experienced in dealing with abductees do have a tendency not to be as ethically minded as they should be. In fact, many abductees that I have spoken to feel that many within the UFO community do not view them as people requiring help but rather as a source of raw data on the subject. This is a tough line to tread for the abduction therapist/researcher but surely the primary function is to help the abductee come to terms with what they might have experienced and help them integrate their experiences so they can lead as normal a life as possible?

The John Carpenter Affair

Many of the more famous and well-regarded names in alien abduction research have been found to some lesser or greater degree to have poor regard for the aftercare of the abductees they have worked with. John Carpenter was a hypnotherapist who worked with many abductees including Leah Hayley. Rumours started to circulate that Carpenter had sold a number of files detailing information about abductees he had worked with to businessman Robert Bigelow. Bigelow has had a well publicised interest in UFOs and it was claimed that Carpenter sold 140 case files to Bigelow for $14,000. In a blog post over at The UFO Trail[9] Carpenter claimed that he had never sold the case files, using the ambiguous phrase "data sharing" instead. However, Jack Brewer of the UFO Trail obtained a letter detailing that Carpenter had in fact sold the 140 case files to Bigelow.

Whilst the blog page gives a full account of the saga, which is worth reading, the main point to take away for our purposes is that abductees who had partaken in hypnotic sessions with Carpenter were under the impression they were dealing with a mental health professional, yet the reality was that the boundaries between patient and therapist were very unclear and ill-defined, resulting in underhand deals and ill-fated legal cases. Many of the abductees had felt extremely violated and had little recourse. Whether the Carpenter was a good therapist is now a moot point as his aftercare was found to be woefully lacking.

The Emma Woods Incident

---

[9] http://ufotrail.blogspot.com/2013/10/the-carpenter-affair-for-record.html

Emma Woods (not her real name) is an alleged abductee from New Zealand. Emma is a middle-aged woman, who claimed to have experienced phenomena which has led her to believe that something very strange was happening to her. On her sadly now defunct website, Woods wrote eloquently on her experiences and documented her interactions with one of alien abductions leading researchers, David Jacobs.

David Jacobs, retired associate professor of History at Temple University, is known for his dark portrayals of the abduction phenomena. Books such as *"The Threat. The Secret Alien Agenda: What the Aliens Really Want ... And How They Plan to Get It"* or *"Walking Among Us: The Alien Plan to Control Humanity "*, leave the reader under no illusion that Jacobs believes the abductor's intentions are far from benevolent. The same could be said for his treatment of Emma Woods, whose experience highlighted the real minefield that alien abduction research has clumsily wandered into.

Jacobs began conducting hypnotic regression with Woods via international telephone calls. Now, while I accept it is possible to hypnotically regress someone via a telephone call, at some point common sense must kick in and ask whether this is a safe approach. The safety of your patient is paramount and hypnosis via phone line is not a safe approach. Also, how do you really know that your patient is hypnotised? How can you adequately deal with a potentially traumatised patient over a phone line?

As the Wood/Jacobs patient/therapist relationship grew, Jacob's behaviour veers dramatically into dark territory. Jacobs tells Wood that she has Multiple Personality Disorder (MPD). Not that Jacobs has any actual evidence of this or has the mental health training to adequately diagnose such a complex condition, but Jacobs has allegedly told her this to fool any alien/hybrid who might be interfering with Woods. Again, ethically speaking, at no point should you be planting such notions into a patient's head. Is it any wonder that sceptics will continue to argue that alien abduction researchers do nothing but lead their patients into accepting their own beliefs and ideas? Jacob's suggestions lurch from being dark and unethical to weird, creepy and unethical.

Due to the sexual nature of some of Woods' experiences, Jacobs suggests (in all seriousness) that she buys and wears a chastity belt to avoid any sexual interference from her alleged abductors. In another session Jacobs suggests that Woods sends him a pair of her underwear, presumably for analysis.

The more you dig into the story you soon become aware that there was a lot of weirdness from both parties and that both parties are far from innocent in all of this. For example, Woods sent a message to Jacobs via AOL Messenger purporting that it came from an alien hybrid, then changed the story claiming she wrote the message in a deep sleep state. Alarm bells should have been ringing loud and clear highlighting that a firm scientific method for researching these cases is what is required.

At what point is Jacob's behaviour scientific or ethical? If Jacobs had any mental health training, he would have been able to deal with some of Wood's bizarre behaviour in a more professional manner. This type of poor research is why sceptics view UFOs and alien abduction as nothing more than people trying to make a few dollars or massage their own egos.

Of course, the other elephant in the room regarding the Woods saga is that Jacob's holds no qualifications in hypnosis or psychotherapy. He claims to have helped 150 patients regarding claims of alien abduction yet holds no qualifications. I acknowledge there is no training that would prepare anyone for dealing with claims of alien abduction, but basic training in hypnosis and psychotherapy as a minimum must surely be a prerequisite? Of course, this must lead us to question Jacob's previous work prior to his work with Emma Woods, because as we have seen, his approach is lacking any form of competence. Recordings of Woods and Jacobs interactions can be listened to at Jack Brewer's The UFO Trail blog[10].

Surely with the issues raised by incidents such as this, if we include the claims from Carol Rainey and other observers, aren't we at a point where the whole phenomena needs some re-appraisal as well as much more research especially focussing on a framework for helping those who have claimed to been abducted? Sadly, those who do offer

---

[10] http://ufotrail.blogspot.com/2015/08/mufon-sham-inquiry-and-woodsjacobs.html

good quality support to alleged abductees often do not get the credit they deserve. By not looking into the state of alleged abductee support and research we enable the continuation of bad practice and poor science. As many abductees demonstrate symptoms of PTSD, many of the practices within PTSD treatment would fit perfectly for assisting abductees to come to terms with their experiences and surely these would be a better start than jumping straight into hypnosis?

5 ALIEN ABDUCTION: THE OVERVIEW

For many experiencers, it might only be a single weird experience, dream or situation that can often open up an avalanche of other memories of experiences and strange encounters that indicate these experiences may have been ongoing throughout their entire life.

For many, encounters with aliens may have started in early childhood. People often have memories of encountering strange little people, or maybe entities perceived as ghosts or spirits, balls of light or strange adult sized beings (sometimes very human-like). Often the mood is playful and almost parental or avuncular. These childhood visitations are usually accompanied by bright lights shining into bedrooms, strange humming noises and associated vibrations, and often other strange poltergeist-like activities. Often these childhood encounters are coupled with sightings of UFOs, sensations of flying, floating through their house, and finding themselves in strange rooms, usually with other beings.

There seems to be a palpable change as the experiencer hits puberty as the encounters become more about painful procedures and as the experiencer develops further there seems to be a more sexual element to a lot of the encounters.

It appears that abductions can run along family lines and looking at published accounts these encounters can go back to several generations. There are even some accounts where children have encountered parents on-board craft. However, often the parent might have no recollection of the event.

It appears that abductions encounters occur through an abductees/experiencer's life, but there is no discernible pattern as to when or why these events occur. It is often claimed that events occur during periods of stress or inner development. Alternatively, it might be that these periods of stress or growth may make the memories more accessible to the experiencer.

It has been observed that certain fears or phobias that develop for the experiencer may be a side-effect of abduction events. Abductees often report a fear of medical procedures or implements such as syringes, a profound fear of the dark (often resulting in sleeping with the light on in adulthood), fear of certain animals or insects, fear of enclosures or non-descript rooms, and issues around sexual contact.

Physical indicators also become noticeable during the abductee's lifetime. There is a lot of evidence that scrapes, scoop marks, unusual rashes, recurrent nose bleeds and unusual cuts are noticeable by abductees as indications that something unusual might have happened. Often, for female abductees, menstrual, reproductive, and gynaecological issues may arise.

Abductees often report that electrical devices and equipment start to misbehave, malfunction or just completely fail especially directly after abduction experiences.

Independent witnesses or evidence is rarely found that would confirm the reality of an abduction event taking place. In many of the published cases, abductees recall seeing family members on-board craft but they seem to be in a trance like state, often noted that they looked like they were "switched off", but the family member has zero recollection of the event.

In cases such as the Allagash Four, the Calvin Parker incident or Garry Wood and Colin Wright's incident, there have been others involved to corroborate the story. In the case of the Linda Cortile abduction, there were several witnesses who allegedly reported seeing the abduction take place. Also, there were several independent witnesses who reported seeing a UFO in the vicinity of Linda's apartment the evening of the abduction. A neighbour of Linda's reported seeing an eerie light illuminate the courtyard of the building on the night of the abduction. Furthermore, another abductee, "Marilyn Kilmer" reported that she had previously been abducted with Linda. Linda and Marilyn were able to independently verify what each other was wearing during this experience.

It is a phenomena that seems to exist in our everyday third dimensional reality but somehow also exists in realms where the certainties, constraints and understandings of our consensus reality and the general laws of physics are not acknowledged. In the case studies that follow we will see people taken into a personal journey that makes very little sense to them, that will push them into the very extremes of understanding and knowledge and will deconstruct just what it is to be a human. This phenomenon will also deconstruct everything we understand in terms of how the universe works and our place in it.

How can people go on these incredulous journeys and not bring 'something' back to the everyday reality of human existence as we generally experience it? Such experiences leave scars, both physically, mentally and on a soul level. Is it possible to bury the experience and remain chained to the everyday existence that we all participate in? It seems not for many abductees/experiencers.

All the experiencers that I have met have demonstrated signs of Post Traumatic Stress Disorder (PTSD) but have also demonstrated signs of Post Traumatic Growth (PTG), where artistic, philosophical and spiritual endeavours suddenly become more important and blossom. That statement does not exist to justify the pain, suffering and torment that many abductees/experiencers experience, but it seems that both PTSD and PTG are two sides of the same coin that is the currency of experiencers of alien abduction.

Many religions point to suffering as a portal to spiritual growth and many artists point to suffering as the catalyst for creating their most inspired work. Is this PTG a chance side-effect or is it something that is co-created with the abductors? Many abductees speak of "contracts" they have agreed to with their abductors in previous lifetimes. How likely is this? Is this a belief implanted by the abductors to justify their actions? Is the PTG the experiencers/abductees' payment in return for giving the abductors what they need? Speaking of past-life contracts is difficult territory for many abductees who feel the incursion of their abductors is deeply disturbing and was uninvited. How and why would you agree to the schism that is created in your life? But as with all aspects of alien abduction, understanding is difficult to come by. This is a phenomena that lurks in the reaches of human experience we are least equipped to access, understand or deal with.

The following case studies show that not only does the abduction phenomena sometimes deviate from the "cookie-cutter" experience occasionally, but that there are many people who have very clear memories of their experiences.

Only by listening to the experiencers/abductees can we get closer to an understanding of this phenomenon and the truly reality changing implications of this phenomena intervening with humanity is this way. The following case studies are documented without the use of hypnosis.

6 CASE STUDY #1 - MIKE

It only takes a short stroll from the hectic streets of Oxford Circus to find yourself amongst the slightly more sedate and bohemian streets of Soho. London is a collection of worlds within worlds. Layers of reality seemingly overlaid upon each other to make the whole reality make sense. I am meeting Mike, a merchant banker, who has tried to flee his lifetime of alien abduction experiences by "hiding" in London. I meet Mike in a dimly lit coffee shop in the heart of Soho. Mike leans back in his chair, his features barely visible in the dark corner of the shop. "It's a cliché, but you can run but you can never hide. They will find you, you are a marked man or woman."

Mike's experiences started in the early 1970's, as a child in Yorkshire. "I remember how small balls of shimmering blue light would drift into my bedroom from outside. I would stare transfixed as these glowing orbs would effortlessly float in the middle of my bedroom, just hovering and shimmering. In my limited way I would try and explain this to my parents, but in a typically Yorkshire working-class fashion such flights of fancy were soon put to rest.

"Things turned a little more serious when my parents started to become aware of episodes of missing time. When I was about six years old we went on holiday as a family. We were staying in a cottage in Devon. My parents recall that suddenly I wasn't there. Completely disappeared! They looked around the cottage but I was nowhere to be seen. They started hunting around near the cottage, thinking I might have managed to get out. After two hours of searching, which did involve the police, I magically appeared in the cottage. And I do mean magically appeared. My parents found me in my bed as they searched the cottage for the umpteenth time. Now, my parents are not going to miss a child in the bed. My parents were so confused. They searched that house many times. They started to suspect there was something very weird going on. It wasn't long after this that my experiences started to change.

"My night-time experiences started to become more intense with entities actually being present in my room. They looked like the stereotypical Grey alien, although at that time and that age I had no concept of 'aliens'. As far as I was concerned, they were just weird people who regularly turned up in my bedroom. Even though they all look identical, you do know them as individuals. Not as if they all have names, but you learn their energy. You certainly 'know' if they had been with you previously. That energy is also tied up with their job or their role. The doctor or the educators have a different energy to the beings that take you from home to their craft. The escorts, as I called them, have almost an irreverent attitude at times. But all of them are so job focused. Nothing else mattered other than completing that job or task. At times, it felt very robotic.

"I was very aware, and my parents were to some extent, that I was having some intense experiences. Beings were taking me to a craft on a very regular basis. Often, several times a week. It was like I was being educated on some of these visits. We hadn't moved on to the physical examination stuff yet, so it was all still kind of fun and interesting. I would be there with other children, not a huge amount of children, but small groups of six or seven and we would watch holograms of nature, stuff about politics and stuff about space. The whole time these beings would stare at us to gauge our reactions. They were trying to feel how we felt about what we were seeing. In some regards it was an exciting and inspiring time as we were having all this information downloaded into us. Information that would bubble up in later life. These experiences happened before things got really dark and confusing.

"As I moved into my later teens, 16, 17, 18 years of age, the experiences started to focus more on the physical aspects of my life. The fun interaction and education times were seemingly over. There was one time when my parents were away on holiday, and I was home on my own. It was late evening, around 9pm and dark outside. I had this annoying feeling that there was something outside in the back garden. Part of me was wanting to investigate and part of me knew that there was something going to happen if I went outside. The nagging feeling started to become a metaphorical scream in my head. I had just got to go and look. I tentatively opened the back door and stepped onto the patio. Immediately I was surprised to see a typical grey alongside a tall Nordic type alien. The Nordic was very tall, at least six and a half feet and very muscular. He has long, straight blonde hair. The hair was very light, almost white in colour and blue eyes which seemed to almost sparkle very intensely. His eyes felt as if they were looking into your soul and he was understanding everything about you. I got the strong sense as if he was in some way 'reading' me. I almost jumped out of my skin but suddenly had reassurances floating into my mind. Everything was going to be OK, they meant no harm and I was to trust them. Which probably wasn't totally correct.

"The Grey seemed lifeless, almost machine-like, just standing there until the Nordic alien grabbed my left wrist and pulled my left arm outwards so it became straight. His grip was vice-like. I wasn't going to wriggle free of that grip. The Grey alien lifted its arm to show it had something akin to a wand, with a glowing tip. On that tip was a very small cube of what looked like metal. The Grey alien placed the tip of this wand on my left wrist and this flat-ish cube was left on my wrist. The object then started to gently burrow into my skin. It almost vibrated slightly, gently moving left to right to worm its way under my skin. When it had fully disappeared, the Nordic released my arm. The skin formed back around where the object had entered. Still to this day, I have a small square scar on my wrist."

Mike pulls up the sleeve of a very expensive looking monogrammed shirt to show me the scar. It was perfectly square, about 3mm each side and a slightly lighter shade of pink than the rest of the skin around it.

"Once the cube had disappeared, they seemed really pleased with themselves and we all looked for a moment at the pink scar that was forming on my wrist. Now they had released my wrist and told me to go back inside. Which I duly did as if this was the most normal thing in the world. I just went back to normality as if nothing had happened.

"I was now driving around this time and would often get the urge to pop out for a drive, only to end up chasing a strange light in the sky and then arriving home with a huge amount of missing time. Strangely, you fail to question it fully. It is almost as if you've become primed to accept and normalise something that is obviously not very normal. It is almost like there are thoughts implanted in your mind that stop you rationally analysing certain events. It was just normal for these things to happen. I think that is why many experiencers are unaware of some or even all of their experiences. Their minds accept it, compartmentalise it, and then they just carry on.

"These orbs were very constant in all my experiences. Whatever they were, I could not really say with any certainty, but one experience left me feeling they were some kind of machine, but with some form of consciousness. I was still living with my parents around this time and one evening I remember being unable to sleep, I was really very restless. Suddenly an orb materialised in the corner of my bedroom. It was a cool blue colour and it hovered silently, the blue colour sometimes shimmering and sometimes appearing slightly duller in colour. I suddenly felt a weight on my chest, almost as if something was holding me down. I could really feel this very physical pressure on me. This orb then moved a little closer. In my mind it felt as if it was partly observing me and partly trying to find something out, almost as if scanning me for some information. It felt like I was pinned down for ages but in reality, it was probably just a few minutes. I was a little panicky as this seemed very direct and intrusive. We had moved on from playful, chasing shadows-type experiences into more intense and direct encounters.

"Once the object had done whatever it had to do it shot off to the right and disappeared through the wall. As it moved through the wall near the bedroom window, the curtain rippled as if a draft had been caused. Then the pressure lifted on my chest, and I gradually fell asleep. Again, I was internally rationalising that this was all quite normal.

"As I went through University things seemed to calm a little. The experiences seemed to be more sporadic during this time, and I wouldn't say that I had forgotten about them, but it was almost as if a presence in my life had departed, or maybe stepped back a little. But there were a couple of experiences that were reminders to the weirdness that had interwoven itself into my life.

"The first was during a summer job, I was travelling to one of the sites my employer had. I was being driven by a co-worker. It was a typical summer's day, we were travelling on a mountain road when a car suddenly swung out behind us from a layby and started tail-gating us. The other driver was beeping his horn and gesticulating wildly. The driver was in his mid-50s, dressed in a black suit, with a white shirt and black tie, black sunglasses and jet black hair, slicked back. He evidently wasn't happy about something! Anyway, several times he tried to overtake but was thwarted because the mountain road was too narrow.

"A glint in the distance attracted me to the fact that there was a slim saucer shaped object hovering over on the other side of the valley. At the time I thought 'Great! Being tracked by a UFO whilst a weird man-in-black is chasing us!'. The guy who was driving me was doing his best to stay on the road. We reached the outskirts of a small village and planned to lose the other car by sudden turns down random streets, but the other driver was too good to fall for that trick. We found ourselves on a one-way system and were just going around this one-way system in this tiny village for about five minutes. Both cars were just going around and around, no-one able to break out of this weird game of cat and mouse.

"After a few circuits around the one-way system we noticed a small Police station. Our plan was to suddenly swerve into the parking at the front of the station and run in and get some help. So on the next pass, we swerved in, stopped the car in the entrance driveway, jumped out of the car and ran for the Police station. It was sudden enough that the other driver was caught off guard.

"He continued on the one-way system, so we knew we had a couple of minutes to recount the situation to whoever was in the station. We were half-way through this story to the desk officer when the guy who had been chasing us walked in. He has an air of authority, he seems very calm and centred, but there is something slightly otherworldly about him. Something about him just doesn't seem right. He is your archetypal man-in-black. So, the officer literally puts us in a cell so the guy chasing us can have a chat with him.

"Ten minutes later the officer comes in and berates us for wasting everyone's time. No mention of this guy chasing us, nothing. The man in black is nowhere to be seen. We return to work, quite late, and I am wanting the ground to open up and swallow me because this just all feels too weird and it's affecting other people now.

"However, after University things started to really escalate again. I'd managed to get a job in local government, basically crunching numbers. I was driving to the local station to catch a train to work. It's a lonely road, and again a car appeared from nowhere with a man and a woman driving it. They kept really close to me on the road. As I pulled into the station and parked, they chose to park right next to me in a totally empty car park. They got out, one guy and one woman, and they looked almost identical. They looked like brother and sister, all dressed in black, with dark glasses and dark hair. They were wearing dark glasses at 6.30 in the morning on a dark winter day. The guy looks across to me and says, 'Any sign of the Feds?'.

"I had no idea what to say to that. What did that actually mean? Was this a reference to the other man-in-black incident? So, I ignored the questions and I quickly walked to the platform. They followed and stood just a few feet from me. I waited for what seemed like an age. I just didn't want to engage with them. They just stood and stared, impassively. When the train finally arrived, I got on and sat down. The people in black walked to the edge of the platform, right up close to the train and just watched me until the train pulled away. This type of weirdness comes in waves and is part and parcel of experiencers lives. It makes no sense.

"There were still a lot of sightings going on around me. It was becoming very intense. There were two incidents that forced me to make some serious changes in my life. The first incident was extremely troubling. I was lying in bed, but I was unable to sleep, something was troubling me. I got to know when 'they' were around, I just knew. I went downstairs to get a drink. Then what I thought was my girlfriend followed me downstairs.

I watched what I thought was her descend the stairs, but as she was half-way down the stairs, I just knew for some reason it wasn't her and as soon as I came to that conclusion 'it' changed its appearance to this other person, who was totally naked. It or She now looked like a blonde-haired woman, short cut hair and a perfect body. No human has a body like this. It was too perfect. Everything was sculpted to perfection making the being look unreal. Every muscle and fold of skin was perfectly sculpted. I found myself feeling very aroused, something unseen was causing this arousal and when she approached me every nerve in my body was pulsing with energy. I have never felt that alive or connected and haven't since. The whole time I was aware I was being manipulated to feel this way, but I couldn't seem to fight it.

"We had sex immediately. It was mind-blowing but again, I was very aware I was somehow being manipulated. Once I had finished, she stood up, stepped a few paces away and pulled out a clear container from within her vagina. Within the container was my sperm. The whole episode had been constructed by this intelligent machine, which was able to change its appearance based on what I thought. It was able to manipulate my body and mind with the sole purpose of obtaining a sample. It looked at me in an impassioned way and then literally disappeared like someone suddenly pressed a button. I suddenly became aware of a noise outside, and nervously peered through the curtains. Outside I saw two black clad figures walking down the road away from the house. They were walking in perfect unison, in a very mechanical fashion, almost painfully robotic.

"Tiredness suddenly overcame me and I returned to bed. I couldn't wake my girlfriend; she was out cold. I soon fell asleep. The following day I was wracked with guilt. Technically I had cheated on my girlfriend. I wasn't sure what exactly I had slept with, but I had just had sex with someone or something other than her. I was devastated, but I could never really explain.

"Later that day I was talking with one of my neighbours, the usual everyday chit-chat and they explained that they had come home from a night shift and witnessed a small saucer shaped object over the housing estate I lived on. They said they stood and watched it for a couple of minutes as it hovered there totally silently, then suddenly, just like someone flicking a switch, it was gone.

"These experiences were starting to involve too many people and I was afraid people were going to hurt in some way or another. I decided to move to London and, in effect, try to hide away from this. You can't hide but you can avoid dragging other people into it. At least that was my very naive thinking.

"I have learnt to compartmentalise my experiences, not to try to integrate them into the rest of my life. I couldn't or wouldn't want to. Nine to five, I am a successful banker, and after those hours a lot of weird stuff happens and providing that both worlds don't collide then I am relatively happy. I can't stop these experiences, no-one can adequately explain these experiences, so I have to manage them as best I can. I have no real understanding of what these experiences mean and I think, having spoken to some other experiencers, I don't really think they have an understanding of the total picture. In these experiences, it appears that we the experiencer, abductee, call it what you will, is only allowed to see what they are supposed to see. They are only allowed to experience what they are supposed to experience. Not for our benefit, of course, but for theirs. So, everything is expertly stage-managed by them so the experiencer or abductee only sees what is centre-stage, and never allowed to see how and why the whole show is being performed. There is certainly no backstage access.

"Is this positive for me? No. It has ruined relationships, I have lost friends, I had to move away to protect a lot of things because people do not get it, or rather they get it in a small Hollywood way of aliens and cool spaceships, but this is also much more about human identity and interacting with something much bigger than ourselves, and the dangers and pressures this brings to some experiencers. The pressure to make sense of this is huge. The dangers are not being able to manage the amount of inner journeying you have to take to try to piece yourself back together so you can function as a human. It also creates a distance between you and other people because you don't want to have to transfer all this weight of experience on to them. I judge myself as one of the lucky ones, as I have met others who have had far more difficult experiences, far more complex dynamics in regard to their waking lives. As an experiencer you often feel as if you are on a string. You will get moved into situations as if dragged by an invisible string. People will come into your life as if they have been moved by an unseen force. You sometimes feel as if you are their puppet, in a story that you never will understand.

"One of the first experiences I had when I moved to London illustrated that this is part of a bigger game, for want of a better word, when I was still finding my way around the city. I had been idly wandering around the Victoria area one night and a man stopped me asking for directions. I confessed to being a stranger to the city. Then the guy smirked and said, 'you are no stranger to me'. He put his hand out, palm facing me and placed it on my heart. Instantaneously I was having all these memories of previous experiences all rushing back into my mind, things I had previously forgotten. Then suddenly I was on this craft, and we were flying over London, and I had this amazing view of the city from the sky. The bottom of the craft seemed to be transparent, and we were flying at leisurely pace over central London, obviously oblivious to the people below. Two greys appeared beside me and led me away to a side-room where I was introduced to a taller grey. He stared into my eyes and it felt like he was reaching into my mind, looking for those new memories that I had remembered. We briefly connected and almost remembered them together, as if we were sharing this memory in a symbiotic fashion, which resulted in a strange camaraderie after he stopped looking into me. Almost as if he had now integrated them into his own memories as raw material. He titled his head and I felt almost like a sense of love that one would have towards a small child or a small animal. He was almost amused by the purity of the shared experience. He then said, telepathically, 'Our connection is what you ultimately all crave'.

"I found myself back on the street, feeling very emotional and very bemused. The streets were deserted, and I estimate I had been gone for around an hour. A few days later I was at a conference connected with my job and I got chatting to some woman from what I assumed was a competitor bank. We stood at these huge windows overlooking part of the Thames and across to the hustle of the city across the water. She cryptically said 'You're such watchers, you humans. But we'll keep an eye on you. Always', and smiled broadly. She turned and looked deep inside me, in only a way they can. She walked away swiftly towards the toilets. I stood there almost shaking. A normal looking human came up to me and said something that chilled me to the core with a simple and innocuous statement, because she obviously knew something. I later asked the organisers and nobody really seemed to know who she was or where she was from, but obviously she had enough of a background story to get into this conference. The bigger picture of this phenomena is deeply complex. It's not all cool aliens and cool spaceships. This is very deep and very serious, as they evidently walk among us."

Mike takes a moment to compose himself. It seems like he has unloaded a lot of things from his mind and almost looks a little unsettled. He adjusts his cuffs and tie. He straightens up in the seat and I watch as he transforms himself, metaphorically, from experiencer to banker. His demeanour changes. He swallows the last of what must now be a cold cup of coffee. "I must be going. I try not to linger in one place for too long. You have to keep moving, in this life and any others you might be leading."

Mike strides out of the coffee shop and loses himself in the tourist crowds of London as he walks to the financial centre of the City, again walking between various worlds.

7 CASE STUDY #2 - TINA

The smell of incense, the tie-dye clothing and the abundance of crystals on rings and necklaces gives the first impression of a typical hippie/new-ager, but once Tina opens her mouth all pretence to 'love and light' is gone. Tina is a self-styled cosmic warrior and is under no illusion as to what she sees is at the heart of the abduction phenomena.

"It's a spiritual war, my friend. It's a physical war, it's a war for resources, it's a war on all levels and all dimensions, and too few people are fighting it. Too many people are blinded by the glitter and gleam of so-called reality and do not see what is actually going on around them. You have masters, on this plane of existence and on other planes of existence. I have seen these planes of existence through my UFO encounters, and I have encountered these so-called masters, who themselves have masters, and so one and so forth, as in a never ending cycle of reality there is always another level and another entity trying to pull someone else's strings. There is a war on this planet, but we're distracted by day to day trivialities. But I digress."

Tina has temporarily stepped down from her soapbox and begins in a more calm fashion to recount how her "war" had begun. "As a child I seemed to read people and know when things were going to happen. Some would say I was very psychic. Everyone said that I was an old soul trapped in a young body. It seemed like a cute thing to say about a child, but I soon learnt to hide that side of myself from others. Other people like to feel like the smartest person in the room, and their ego and their arrogance opens a door so you can peer inside and see them for who they are. It was a game I soon developed, just letting someone open their innermost secrets to me and all I had to do was let them massage their own ego. As a child I was quickly aware of other levels of reality. I saw fairies, I saw the spirits of dead people, so I was very aware that what you see is not always what you get. This reality is all around us. But you soon learn to keep quiet because no-one wants to hear that information. Very few people want to consider that we are trapped in a very base version of reality. The more advanced souls can often see more levels of reality, how those levels interact and sometimes where they intersect.

"My first conscious encounter was around the age of 8. I had been aware for a little while that there was 'something' around me. A sense of an energy that seemed to want to stay hidden. But one day, as I played with some friends in the nearby park, I soon spotted a small figure standing near the edge of the treeline. It looked like the stereotypical Grey-type alien. There was a small wood on the edge of the park and as kids we concocted stories that there were magical creatures in there, or evil witches lived there, so it tended to put the other kids off straying into there. The small being sensed I had become aware of it, and it started to slowly move deeper into the woods, silently encouraging me to follow. I just could just feel it drawing me in. I slowly drifted out of the game we were playing, the other kids not really noticing I was walking away. I followed the being, always just staying close to see it but not too close as I wasn't sure of it yet. I sensed a playful energy but there was something else. I felt like I was being teased. Part of me hinted that this was a trap with the small being playing as bait, but once I began to think that it was like someone turned up the amplifier on the playful vibes to obscure the intuition. Classic distraction!

"We had walked almost through the woods to a field on the other side. The field was steep and on the ridge of the field was a small craft, silver, like brushed metal. The being was now with several other beings. I suddenly felt like I knew these creatures, that I was once one of them, or maybe once part of them and now I was different. It was a curious experience. I think that there is almost like a hive consciousness with a lot of the Greys, especially the smaller ones, so you can quite easily pick-up on what messages are swirling around them. They recognised me on one level, but knew I was now different. I came up the hill and the playful vibe was strong again. They worked hard to keep my mind busy so I couldn't see or understand everything that was going on that day.

"We entered the ship and suddenly I got the sensation of a deep bass-like hum which I took to indicate we were moving. A quick wave of panic hit me. Despite my young age I understood that I had put myself in danger as no-one knew where I was. The Greys picked up on that and reassurance and happy vibes were beamed my way. They needed me to be compliant. We were standing in a central room, curved, no furniture and nothing to give you any bearings of where you were. A table came up through an opening in the floor and I was lifted, by something, onto the table. I felt a gentle pressure on my shoulders, just enough to encourage me to stay led down, but not painful. Then a couple of the taller greys appeared. They almost swept in and the smaller beings stood back, you could almost feel the reverence they had towards the larger beings. These taller beings were obviously the leaders of this little mission.

"One of them came forward and stared deep into my eyes. I tried to look away but couldn't. This tall grey was reading my mind, not looking for anything in particular I believe, but was just peering in and it felt like he was trying to establish a connection. Which he achieved. It was almost like pairing a Bluetooth device! If he was in my vicinity, he was connected. He could now feel how I felt. He stepped back and another one came forward with what appeared to be a syringe. It was silver, you could not discern any liquid within it. It was stuck in my arm and it really stung. The first tall Grey put his hand on my forehead and the pain subsided instantly. There was that connection in action! His hand felt limp, and cold, the sort of coolness you get when you touch marble or polished granite. It felt dead as we might understand it. No energy, no real life-force to it. Suddenly the pressure from my shoulders was removed and I was lifted off the table. The tall Greys scuttled away and one of the small beings led me down a corridor. I walked but he seemed to float in front of me. We stopped by a room with glass walls. Within the room were other human women. There were around eleven in total, and they were all cradling what I thought were young babies. Amazing, I thought! Childcare in space! But as I had more experiences, I came to understand these children were some form of hybrid and these hybrids needed that human connection. They needed that emotional connection. It's an energetic requirement they have, they get food and liquids where they are but they need that energetic connection to help them develop. They develop their side of the genetic heritage that humans provide through regular contact. However, genetics is not an exact science when it comes to the soul level but that is another story."

"I continued down the corridor and was led into a room with a huge screen. The screen seemed to float in the air but very close to the wall, I couldn't see any attachments. As I looked at the screen it came to life. It showed footage of a desert world, where people had to live underground. There were humans and Greys underground together. Then there were scenes of a beautiful paradise. There was no music, just the background hum I experienced earlier. The scenes kept alternating, desert world, then paradise, desert world then paradise. On and on it went and I soon got bored. Whatever the message of this, it passed me by. But as soon as I got really bored and distracted the screen would shut off. There was suddenly an urgency to get me out of the room and back into the corridor. I was again following this short Grey and it explained to me that I had to go home. I found myself sliding down a tube of light with the being and I literally landed on my ass on the field. Which this being found amusing in its own way. I felt it say goodbye, and I sensed it was going to miss me. I felt very conflicted here. This was weird, they were weird, and I hadn't asked for this, but I felt part of them, and they knew this. It was a mixture of emotions. But I got up and ran through the woods to find my friends still playing the games I had left them playing. They suddenly noticed me and asked where I went. I played dumb and said I had been here all the time. We returned to playing as that's what kids do. We bury things and try to get back to normal. But once that door to alternate realities is open, you can never fully close it.

"When I was home later that day the stinging sensation returned to my arm and there was a red bruising to that part of the arm. I still felt conflicted as I started to feel I had been duped in some way. Later experiences taught me to value those intuitive feelings when you are alone or can centre yourself. There were some alarm bells ringing for me and I was starting to listen.

"After this incident there was a lot of poltergeist activity within my house. Weird little things happening, often playful in nature but it was as if this energy was just reminding me that 'they' were still here even though I couldn't see them.

"Their visits would be very regular, they wanted to mesh themselves into my life so I would accept them as the norm, that's how I feel in retrospect. They wanted me to feel that they were my family. As much as I loved my flesh and bones family, I felt a stranger with them. They weren't like me in many ways, and that isn't a criticism and these beings I was encountering filled a void in my life.

"I became more aware of my experiences as time went on. I became really hard-wired and fine-tuned as to when they were around. In later life, my cats are always aware first or seem to know when the Greys will be around. They get very skittish, very uneasy. They stare at things that I cannot see, and you know they are watching something. It is just a presence, a feeling, it's like I can detect them like an energetic connection. In my teens I shared an experience with a friend, and it was the start of when my experiences made me feel as if I was being treated less of an equal and more of a laboratory subject.

"I walked to school every day, and I walked in with my friend Sandra. We would meet after school and would walk home together. Sandra was a year older than me. One day, we were walking near the park I told you about when we both noticed this black object far above us. It looked like a black circle in the sky. The blackness against the blue sky made it look like there was an actual hole in the sky. The black object started to descend as it was now gradually getting bigger. Sandra and I both stood rooted to the spot and we could feel our bodies starting to vibrate. It was like there was an electrical current flowing through us. As we kept looking up a large clear sphere appeared under the black object. The black object looked as if it was just hovering now, and this clear sphere was now descending towards us.

"We stood there, quivering with all this energy flowing through us, and this sphere came down and enveloped us. We felt a slight tingling sensation as this sphere, basically, surrounded us. Then, as if it was solid, we started rising into the sky towards the black object. It was like we were rising in a clear sphere or bubble.

"Sandra was terrified, she was screaming hysterically. Who could blame her? We were now picking up speed and approaching the black object and then suddenly we were inside it. We became aware that we were in a large room, with lots of metallic tables. On those tables were humans. There were about twenty beds in total. All the humans, both men and women, were led down and were being attended to by a large Grey and a smaller Grey at each table. At the far end of the room was a much larger reptilian creature. It was just watching, impassively. There were also tall Nordic ETs walking between the tables, as if keeping an eye on things, maybe observing, who knows? We were shown to two vacant tables. I remember leaning up against the table and it was ice cold to the touch. We were encouraged to sit on the tables, which we did, irrespective of the cold.

"Sandra started to get agitated again, especially when the larger grey started to fiddle with her clothing. It was trying to get to her navel, and Sandra was getting more and more agitated. The larger Grey stared deep into her eyes and Sandra's body became floppy, her face looked relaxed, and the larger Grey was able to remove her clothes and start examining her. I knew it would be my turn next. I surrendered to it. I remember thinking that I needed to understand as much as possible and fighting, at this point, would be counterproductive. I remember them using a long, pointy wand-like device to touch various parts of my body. I remember looking across to other tables and seeing a man with this large cup across his pelvis. The Nordic alien must have noticed me looking. He spoke to me, not telepathically, but verbally "We make checks on humans. We worry about humans, but it also helps us understand things too". He had a strange accent, not quite Germanic, not quite Scandinavian, it had a very hard edge to the accent but a very hard to place yet familiar twang to his accent. I tried to ask what he meant but before I could formulate the sentence, he replied with "Not now. Questions in the future". He smiled, I smiled, he seemed quite nice and genuine. A sharp pinching sensation in my groin brought my attention back to the matter in hand. My groin stung for a while. However, I got the feeling that they were all pleased with whatever it is they were doing. Sandra, on the other hand, was getting agitated again.

"The larger Grey once again stared deep in her eyes and now two of the Nordic ETs moved closer to the table. I don't think there was anything wrong, but I got the impression screaming or crying wasn't what they wanted to deal with. I looked across the room and saw that most of the humans were complying. At the far end there were two other humans in military looking uniforms. Dark green but no markings. They soon left but I have noticed that in a lot of experiences, there is some sort of military usually around. At least, that is my experience.

"The Greys suggested, to both of us, that it was time to go. So, we hopped off the tables and we were escorted out of this room to a very cold corridor. Whilst we walked along the corridor, I could almost sense the hive mind the Greys have. There is almost like constant communication between them all, and I could sense the humans on the craft and how their thoughts and emotions get echoed through the hive. It was a little intense, but it suddenly stopped. Almost as if someone had sensed there was an open channel, and I was listening in.

"We eventually came to another room, where there was a slight breeze. It smelt really fresh, like you have after a storm. It was a curious smell to encounter. Suddenly we were back in this sphere and hurtling back down to the ground. Sandra wasn't screaming this time; she had a haunted look about her. This had been too much for her. We found ourselves back where we started. The sphere just disappeared around us. Sandra sensed we were on solid ground again and sprinted for home. I called after her, but she was too fast. I stood there for a moment, and then began to walk home. When I got home, a fair amount of time had passed. I was probably a few hours later than normal.

"When I spoke to Sandra the next day, she could barely remember the incident. She could remember the UFO sighting, but then she said that we just wandered home. The Greys have very clever ways of clouding the memory. To this day, Sandra has no memory after that sighting. Now, the point is, I was never taken with Sandra again. They don't take people just once or randomly, so I believe Sandra continued to have experiences but does not remember them. I, however, remembered pretty much all of them.

"When I was 19, I fell pregnant. I lost the child due to miscarriage. However, that is the medical story, the Greys took the child as I believe it was a hybrid. Anyway, I had a lot of miscarriages during my twenties and into my thirties. Prior to the miscarriage I would have an abduction-type experience. Now a lot of the time I wasn't really aware if I was actually pregnant, but I would have this miscarriage like experience. The experience that follows would always be the same. I would be taken from wherever I was and I would end up in this medical room. It was always bright white, almost too bright, as if there was a huge amount of light coming through the walls from unseen lights. I would be on a table which was tilted at a slight angle, with my head aimed at the floor. My legs would be on something similar to stirrups and they are giving me an examination similar to a gynaecological exam. There are a few Greys here and once they get whatever they're looking for from inside me, they all leave apart from the taller Grey. I know they have taken something from inside me, but I don't really know what it was. The taller grey then gets closer to me to stare into my eyes and rummage around in my mind and then I'll have a lot of memories resurface. Then it's all over. I get returned.

"These experiences were draining. So, so draining. Not only because I had experienced a particularly tough physical experience, but it was mentally exhausting too. I was trying to fathom out what was happening to me and why it was happening to me. I got to the point where I just had had enough. I just snapped. This was me, my body, my brain, my soul, it's not a commodity for something or someone to help themselves to. So, I decided to fight fire with fire. I launched myself into a massive research project. I had to understand what was happening, where these ETs were coming from and how to protect myself.

"Even though I knew I was having all these experiences prior to me snapping it took a while for me to acknowledge to myself that they were aliens. I mean, to really acknowledge that something from other dimensions is coming into our little world and taking people for their own ends, is a big ask. We know so little about this phenomenon. We truly do. I have spoken to researchers and to other abductees, and we have to agree to knowing so little. Plus, what we do know, we can't take at face value. The Greys are good at messing with people's minds, so nothing can be taken at face value. There is so much manipulation of people's minds.

"I delved into all sorts of occult reading, obscure religious texts, conspiracy theories or conspiracy realities as I refer to them, UFO books, Wicca, anything, I just mentally hoovered it all up. I felt that if I was going to deal with this situation I was going to have to understand reality in its broadest sense, because obviously these Greys were great at bending reality to suit their needs, so I needed to try and level the playing field. As much as you can learn from sacred texts, physics manuals, inner journeying, whatever your path is, you'll soon realise humanity has been kept in the dark and dare I say held back from understanding the greater reality of the universe. Once I realised that, I knew there was no point in wasting any time reading other people's limited understanding. I needed to discover the true nature of reality and the Greys part in it and write the manual for humans to free themselves. My future experiences became opportunities for me to learn about their ways and also disrupt their plans for me. However, the Greys are always interfering in your life and many subsequent experiences taught me that.

"I had just moved to a top floor flat. It was a new housing development, and the rest of the block was currently empty. From the flat I could see across the city, and I would often spend hours watching the city at night. One night I stayed up a little later than usual. It was after midnight. On the horizon a large ball of light appeared. It was a bright light, which would occasionally pulse. It quickly started to move towards me. I remember thinking, strangely with some excitement, 'They're here!' The light sped up and was moving so quickly I thought it would crash into the flat. But it just stopped several feet away. It was like a giant orb, brilliant white. It must have been about 12 feet in diameter. I could feel the hairs on my arm standing up. It felt like there was a huge amount of static electricity in the room.

"Then I saw several figures start to emerge from the orb. It was like they were walking across a bridge of light. They literally walked through the windows into my flat. There was a tall Grey and three smaller Greys. With them was a hybrid looking child. The child looked at me, and slowly walked towards me. If I was judging this as a human child, I suspect it would be about 14 or 15. It looked slender and slightly awkward in its stance. The hair was dark and very wispy. The eyes looked slightly too big for a human, but when I looked at the eyes, they were filled with deep emotion. I could sense feelings of disconnection, of wisdom, hurt, longing, all surging through this strange, fragile creature. The child moved towards me, suddenly and so quickly that I didn't have time to react, and it hugged me. It hugged me so hard. It was almost like a wrestling move; it was that tight. And when I was hugged all this information suddenly started sweeping into my consciousness. It was almost like the life story of this hybrid came flooding into my mind. Along with the realisation that this child was one of mine!

"Now, let us put the brakes on and think about this. Let us go back to the 1950s and 60s, through the 70s, 80s and 90s. Let's think about all those women who were getting abducted and who were having all sorts of reproductive experiments done to them. Those same women were reporting that they were regularly given children to hold. Those same women felt that those children were theirs. Let's think about how many children that could potentially be. Probably a high number. So, the question is: where are all those children? On the planet? Off planet? The implications are huge. The other implications are all those women who have longed after their offspring. Doing that to women is cold. Imagine going through your whole life wondering what became of all those kids you could never talk about. Plus who can you really talk to about this because no-one is ever going to believe you. Even if they did believe you, no-one can do a damn thing. Welcome to helplessness on a galactic scale. But I digress.

"So, there is a huge flood of emotions for me. Firstly, my female and motherly instinct is to feel love and protection towards something that is effectively part of me. There is another part of me that is getting very, very angry as I feel that my emotions are being played with. I feel that this whole episode has been designed to emotionally cripple me for a while. The hybrid and the others obviously are detecting my anger, and I can see them slowly easing back, away from me. The hybrid is trying to calm me. Its thoughts are coming into my consciousness. It can't deal with the anger, it's too dense an emotion. 'Please be calm', she is saying.

"The hybrid, my child, is caught in the middle. It has a connection to me, but it has never known the flipside of being human; the anger, the supposedly "bad" emotions. I am crying now as the full implication of this event is truly hitting home to me. Where are the others they made from me? Why is this happening to me? Why is this happening to us?

Tina takes a moment to compose herself. Wiping away a tear, she breathes deeply and continues. "The hybrid stepped away as the Greys had told her to do so. She can't stay, they said. It's too much for everyone. They turn away and walk towards the orb and disappear the same way they came. The orb disappears just like someone flicked a switch. I fell to the ground and cried and cried, for what seemed like hours. It felt like part of my soul had been ripped out.

"It took me quite a few weeks to get over this particular experience. There is part of me that wonders if that was the reason for it. Maybe they saw I was getting stronger and more bolshie. Maybe they thought an experience like this would knock me back a bit. So, I had to start building myself up again. I needed to start making sure they couldn't get into my mind as easily. I had to start to control my emotions, so others couldn't control them for me.

"I had decided to move and was now living in the country, in quite a remote part. There was about a two mile walk to the nearest village. I found the closeness of nature to be soothing. I would go for long walks as the sun rose. I enjoyed the quiet energy you get then before the energy is disrupted by everyone else going about their business. I was walking through a small, wooded area when I could see a small, silhouetted figure in the pathway ahead. It was about four feet tall, and I could only see this blackness of it as it silhouetted against the light beyond the woods. I continued to walk towards it. As I got close to it, I could see it was a Grey. It had its head cocked at a slight angle; they seem to do this a lot. I could sense it creating a connection with me, and as soon as that connection is there the hive knows about you. I started to block him in a psychic sense, close down the communication. "We are here for you", he said to me telepathically. Not in the sense of support, but in the sense of taking me. "No." I said. And I kept walking. This puzzled him but I kept moving. I walked beyond the Grey. Because I didn't stop, because I kept my emotions in check, because I didn't succumb to fear or anger, I think it put them on the back foot.

"Ahead I noticed two other Greys. I stopped in front of them. I became aware of something off to my right. As I remember it, I turned to look to my right and was aware of this slim silver craft hovering off the ground. It was so highly polished looking it was reflecting the woodland floor on the underside of the object. There was a sudden flash of light, and I couldn't move, it was even difficult to move my eyeballs. The greys converged on me and the next thing I could remember was finding myself on a table. They had removed my clothes, and I was lying face-up on a table. The table was cool, and I felt very uncomfortable. I suddenly feel exhausted, like something is draining my energy, my ability to fight. I am struggling to stay conscious. I felt that drain away from me. A tall Grey leans over and starts to stare deep into my eyes. He's plucking at memories, painful memories, sexual memories, he focuses on anything that generates an intense emotional response. I'm feeling pretty indignant at this point. How dare he help himself to my experiences and feelings!

"Physically, I'm feeling a little numb, but I can feel someone is examining me intimately. I feel instruments being used. They feel slightly cool on my skin. Then suddenly they stop, and the numbness reduces, and I can feel my body again. I am helped up by a couple of smaller Greys. My hybrid child is there at the back of the room, I feel she is happy to see me, but the emotions aren't written on her face. I feel her happiness. I walk to her and she leads me from the room and into a corridor. I feel broken, I feel vulnerable and lost like a child. She is telling me I am strong, that's why I am here. She speaks like the Greys do, in strange sentences that might mean something, that might mean nothing more than placating me. You can never tell. I feel the roles are reversed, she is the mother, the adult and I am the child. I am the naive child in this new reality.

"We move into another room where there is a large window looking out into space. In the distance I can see the Earth, We must be a little bit of a distance away. My mind starts to race and my hybrid daughter detects this. Telepathically she starts talking to me. She tells me that they move away from the earth at times to avoid detection. She states the governments know about them and they avoid causing them [the Governments] too much consternation. An out of sight, out of mind approach. She then becomes more serious.

"Motioning towards the earth she says that things can't go on the way they have been. She is now using her actual voice to speak. It seems very strange to hear, as it is accent-less. Humans don't make sense anymore, she says. We don't understand why you are like you are, she continues. We have tried to understand you, she states. I become confused and ask why this has to be the way it is. Why take people, why hurt them. She feels something approaching sorrow towards me. Not sad that I'm hurting or sad that this happens, but sad that I don't understand and sad that I just can't accept it. The Greys and their hybrids have this huge emotional disconnect. She says that there is so much work to be done. She says that there needs to be much more work for all our futures. She explains there will be a point in the future where events will be taken out of everyone's hands, and we will all be forced to make some big decisions. The future will be unrecognisable to us, she says. She always seems to say a lot but explains little. She says that I have to go, and we will talk more in the future. I remember being pleased for the opportunity to talk in the future but worried about the mental and spiritual cost it might inflict on me.

"I have met many other experiencers or abductees, call them what you will. They are living fractured lives. They are hiding in the shadows because who do you speak to in regard to this? Where is the help? No-one really understands this phenomena with nearly enough depth and nuance. Researchers and experiencers alike. No-one. Yet, there is still a large number of people experiencing terrible things. Terrible physical, mental and emotional things. People are getting scarred by this. It goes on for years. It has been going on for years, and it will continue to go on because it is difficult to stop. These people need help. But from where?

"This is the main issue for me, abductees need help and support. Every day there is that nagging feeling in the back of your head because this phenomena is always there, always lurking, always watching and just waiting to pounce for its own ends. Once you open to that thought all the rest of the thoughts about hybrids, medical procedures, aliens all come rushing in. Mentally, it's exhausting. Physically, it's debilitating. Emotionally it's crippling. So, who you gonna call when the walls between our world and theirs comes tumbling down? That's the daily dilemma. That's one of the daily battles. Holding it all together and peering through our reality to see theirs approaching and trying to fight it off."

8 CASE STUDY #3 - MARCIE

It is tiring hiding big things from people, and it generally is impossible for long periods of time. Hiding an affair or a dubious past can be tiring but hiding a secret so incredible and unbelievable has driven Marcie to the brink of total mental collapse many times. Juggling the requirements of a young and growing family, the duties of a working woman and the pressures of her "shadow-life" has been too much to bear at times.

Marcie claims she is just "ordinary". Marcie explains that she followed the traditional path of "Went to school, got a job, got married, had kids, returned to work". However, a series of events occurred that showed her that what people will judge ordinary is extremely subjective.

"Things unravelled in my life pretty quickly after the incident. Two friends and I had gone to the theatre that night. We had a great night. It was one of those girls' nights out that we had periodically. We were really happy that night, we all had a fantastic time. We were walking back to our car after the show, and we had turned down a street a short distance from the car-park. We were all chatting together, all the usual stuff. We all suddenly noticed that not only was the street unusually quiet, but there was a weird atmosphere. The change was really apparent. There was almost an imperceptible feeling of electricity in the air. The slight, cool breeze had suddenly stopped. There were no traffic noises, there was nothing but silence. Something wasn't right and we could sense it. We started to slow down walking as we felt unsure of our surroundings. It felt so surreal to feel that something was amiss in such a normal, everyday setting. We were looking in all directions, expecting to see something to explain the quiet. Suddenly a figure started to materialise a few feet in-front of us. It was a shimmering outline at first, but quickly the details filled in and there was a solid being a few metres in front of us. It's appearance was like something out of an episode of Star Trek.

"The being looked human and was clothed in a black jumpsuit, which was tight fitting. His footwear seemed to be joined into the jumpsuit, like an all-in-one garment. It highlighted his physique and he appeared quite muscular, but slim. He took a few steps towards us and explained that we needed to accompany him as we had work to do. His demeanour was just so matter-of-fact. Suddenly there was a brilliant flash of light, which took me a few moments to recover my vision from and we found ourselves in a cage with a metallic floor in what appeared to be a huge hangar-type area. It must have been around 100 metres in length and about 50 metres wide. The interior of this area was industrial grey, with slit-type windows towards the top of the walls. We could see nothing but black through the windows. In the hangar were lots of grey cubes, about 10 foot by 10 foot. Some cubes were stacked on top of each other. It just felt like a giant warehouse. At the far end of the hangar were similar cages to ours, with what appeared to be other human looking beings. They were all led down in their cages. We assumed they were asleep. There was a sudden jolt, and we got the sensation we were moving. We could now occasionally see what we thought were stars through the slit-like windows. We were nervous as we had no real idea where we were or what was happening. It still surprises me that we weren't freaking out and shaking the bars of the cage. We soon got very tired, really weary, maybe artificially so and we all led down to sleep. Just like the others.

"Several further significant jolts awoke us and also awoke the other humans in the other cages. We could see a blue sky outside the slit windows, so we knew we had arrived 'somewhere'. Several people in black jumpsuits came into the hangar type area through a door that just literally appeared in the wall. The walls seemed to ripple where the door appeared. There were both women and men in the black jumpsuits. The women were also slightly more muscular than typical human women. Not overly muscular, but more developed in the upper body. The door slid open. They went to the cages at the far side of the hangar and opened the door and motioned the humans to follow one of the people in jumpsuits back through the door. The remaining group of people in jumpsuits walked toward our cage and waved a small hand-held silver cube at the cage door, causing it to open. We were motioned to follow one of the jump-suited people, which we did. We went through the door into a long corridor with corridors running off on both sides of the central corridor. We were guided down one corridor, and we went through an opening at the end which has long strips of thick, heavy plastic hanging down from the top of the door. These plastic strips formed a door you could step through, similar to what you might see at a butchers or a food processing site.

"We walked through into the room which was bathed in a purple bluish light. We were told to undress as we needed to be checked for 'contaminants'. The jump-suited people had no concept of personal space as they just stood there looking at us, intently. We undressed and dropped our clothes to the floor, and one of the jumpsuit people picked up the bundles and put them in a plastic-looking box by the wall. We were told that these clothes would be returned to us later. As we stood there, feeling very vulnerable, a slight hiss was heard, and a gas-like substance came from small gaps in the floor. The purple bluish light started to get more intense. Then suddenly there was a loud click, and the purple light disappeared to be replaced by normal white lighting. The beings in jumpsuits seemed relieved and were looking at each other, smiling broadly. They were smiling as if something good had been achieved. They led us through another door into a room which connected onto a central walkway. We could now see the sky. The walls were floor to ceiling glass, and there were several small, thin trees and bushes within this room. In the corner was an area which had a small wall where you could hide from view. In this area were a number of coloured jumpsuits, similar to what the others wore but a bit more baggy and less well-fitted and we were told to put one on as there would be people coming to see us. We hurriedly put on a jumpsuit not really thinking about what was said to us, but the thought of more people seeing us naked motivated us to comply.

"Once we were dressed, we were told that we could only go behind the wall for short periods of time and we could go there also when the lights went out. The jumpsuit guys went out of the room and the door was shut. There was no visible handle or lock that we could discern. We looked around and noticed that there were other rooms facing ours that were identical. Other people were being led into these rooms, in an identical process to us. So, these rooms were facing each other off a central corridor or walkway. The width of this walkway was about 6 feet and there are several rooms facing ours. Once all the people in black jumpsuits left, the lights dimmed slightly. We slowly walked to the window; we were so perplexed. We also started to feel really tired and mentally foggy. We didn't feel great at all. The people in the other rooms started looking towards us. They looked human. They could have been anyone from any High Street in the world. All white, though. No other ethnicities.

"Suddenly a door opened at the end of the central walkway to our left, and people started walking through. We all recoiled slightly. They looked human, except the clothing was different. Some had coloured jumpsuits, some had what would pass as a skirt or trousers. As humans, they looked too perfect. They were handsome, no flaws, hair perfectly placed, not a spot or blemish in sight. No bags under anyone's eyes. No-one was overweight. All great posture. There was a real intensity in their gaze. When they looked at you, they really burrowed into your soul. They really looked at you and into you.

"The visitors in the walkway were looking into each room. Then it all made perfect sense, we were in a zoo or a living museum. These visitors in the walkway were looking at us as specimens from some far-off place. I told the others my suspicions. Then the panic set in. How long would they keep us here? Our minds were racing as the implications set in.

"After what seemed like a couple of hours, the stream of visitors started to diminish. The lights were starting to slowly dim, almost as if the end of the day was being simulated. This is what the end of a zoo day looks like, we joked. The other humans in the other rooms started to sit down and lie down as if preparing for sleep. This was ridiculous, I thought, and I was becoming very angry but had no idea how to direct this anger. We were still quite scared.

"It was a little while later and no-one was walking through. The door at the back of our room opened and a man in a jumpsuit came through with a metal tray. On it were several bowls of what looked like a smooth grey porridge type substance. The bowls looked metallic and well used. There was a long spatula which I assumed was a type of spoon. I was hungry but also worried. There could be anything in that bowl. We were all looking at each other, worried about taking a bowl. The jump suit guy must have felt our concern. "Look", he said nodding towards the other rooms, "they have been here longer than you and they know it is safe and good for you". We looked across, and true enough the other humans were eating the food. We were still unconvinced. The jump suit guy put the tray on the floor and walked towards the door. I tried to follow but he turned quickly and pointed at me. I felt like a chastised child. I think I actually bowed my head like a naughty child! On reflection, it was weird how we were so subservient, which I put down to this mental fog we were all suffering from. Maybe there was something keeping us calm?

"Anyway, we ate the food, and it tasted a little like porridge, but it was fairly bland. We soon felt sleepy and settled down to sleep on the floor. I slept fitfully that night. After a few hours the lights started to get brighter, again I guess to simulate some sort of daybreak. Then, we sat through another day of people coming to view us and the other humans.

"When the lights started to dim at the end of the day the original guy in the jumpsuit came in through the door. He seemed really happy and said that we could now leave. We dumbly followed the guy, still in this mental fog and wandered behind him towards a room where we found our original clothes. The guy said we were free to get changed. We all quickly got changed irrespective of the fact that the guy was still standing there, watching us.

"Once changed he told us to leave the jumpsuits on the floor. We duly obliged. Once dressed we again meekly followed him into a very small room. The room was very dark. The walls seemed lined with a thick grey material, almost like soundproofing you would see in a recording studio. The air felt very stale. The ceiling seemed to be slightly angled away from us, giving the sensation that the room was shaped towards a point. The guy suddenly seemed to be very still as if he was listening to some voice only he could hear. After a short period, maybe a minute, he seemed to become aware of us again and explained we would be back home shortly. He turned back towards the door and we all became very hazy, almost as if we were drunk, I was desperately fighting to stay conscious. Then the next thing I know I can feel a soft breeze on my face and we are back in the street where this all started. It took a few seconds to fully get my bearings, but I soon noticed the guy was not there at all. No sign of him.

"We walked nervously to the car, really expecting things to be weird. When we got into the car, the clock in the car indicated that we had been gone for only three hours. Which seemed so implausible. But that is what the clock indicated. So, we drove home. In silence, but hyper-vigilant for the next weird thing to happen. We drove home in perfect silence, too afraid to mention any aspect of the event. What else was there to do? Who could you tell this to? When I got home, my husband was furious. He could tell something was wrong and I was being very evasive as to what had happened that evening. I couldn't really explain how I was three hours late. I had no excuse. I didn't feel mentally prepared to concoct a good story. I was like a child saying, "I don't know". This drove a wedge between us for a few days. I just couldn't explain to him. Not just because I was worried about the reaction, but I didn't want to make the experience any more real by verbalising it. Once I spoke about it, it became birthed into the world. I didn't meet my friends for months after for the same reason. We avoided all communication with each other, intentionally, so we avoid making it real.

"After a little while, as I involved myself in everyday tasks, the intense feelings of the event gradually faded, and a sort of normality emerged. I was wishing I could just forget this. Anyway, the mundanity of everyday life seemed to help me forget somewhat, but occasionally there would be weird things happening in the house that would bring it flooding back. My TV would always lose the signal if I got too close to it, weird things like that. So many electrical items would just either freak out or just break down whenever I was around them. But the reality of the whole experience was brought rushing back by another close encounter.

"I was shopping with my husband in town. We were walking down a fairly quiet side street and suddenly, up ahead I saw the guy from my original experience. He is standing in the middle of the street, in his jumpsuit, staring towards me in broad daylight. I grab my husband's arm and shout "That's him!". Admittedly I hadn't told my husband about the experience, so he instantly looked at me in total confusion. I pointed ahead and shouted again "That's him!" but looking up the guy was gone. Suddenly I found myself face down on the pavement. I have no idea what happened, how I got down there but the next thing I know is my husband is leaning over me checking I was ok. I was so confused. I knew I had seen him again but why, and why did I end up face down on the pavement?

"My husband took me to the hospital explaining that I had a fall. My nose was bloodied and I had some bruising and scrapes on my face. I obviously couldn't explain the full story to the hospital staff, so I went along with the story that I had just fallen in the street. My husband knew this was all totally out of character for me and was viewing me with some suspicion during our time in the hospital. Other than a couple of scrapes and bruises I was ok, and the hospital let me go. I then had to explain the whole story to my husband.

"Retelling the whole episode to my husband was cathartic but it ultimately brought the experience more into focus and made it a bit more real. Reliving it raised my anxiety levels through the roof. I had to stop avoiding the two friends who had shared the experience, as I felt we needed to talk. It transpires that my friends had a lot of weird experiences also after the initial experience, but none of them had seen the jumpsuit guy again. Our meeting was a mixture of resharing our experience, many tears and a large amount of bemusement as to what we had really experienced.

"Things settled down for a few weeks after my fall. Thankfully, no weirdness. I didn't think about it too much. I felt like it was all going to be forgotten about. But as I come to learn, that seems to be the time when strange things start to happen again.

"I was at home, getting ready to go out, when I noticed a change in the atmosphere. I could sense almost an electricity in the air. It also felt really dense. Then suddenly these two women in jumpsuits just literally appeared. One was behind me and grabbed me from behind and the one in front of me stared at me. As she did so I started to feel a little tired. The next thing I know, I am on what I assume is a craft of some sort, and we're walking down a bright white corridor. There are blue, rectangular lights set in the wall at waist level. The floor sounded slightly metallic as we walked. The women seemed to have softer footwear on but my shoes clunked a little as we walked.

"We turned into a room with no door. There was a white chair in the middle of the room. It looked like a bigger version of a dentist's chair. I was asked to jump up onto the chair which I did. The chair was really comfy and seemed to fold itself around the contours of my body. Suddenly there was an invisible pressure on my torso and abdomen which was holding me in place, almost as if the chair had grabbed me closer. One of the women lent over me and started staring into my eyes. At first it seemed really oppressive, really invasive, but I started to relax, and her eyes widened slightly as if she was a bit surprised.

"I could feel her in my head, almost like an energy building in my head. Then suddenly lots of images flooded through my mind. Some were from my childhood, but she tended to focus on my sexual memories, replaying some of them several times. I was so embarrassed; they were so personal to me. Then she started to revisit the memories of the original experience I shared with my friends that night. Some of the memories flooded through my mind. Then suddenly it was like she broke the connection and stepped back. She said she was happy, that she had found what she needed and said I should be very proud of myself.

"She walked out leaving me with the other female. The remaining female then started to perform a cursory examination. Checking my eyes, ears and feeling around my throat. She then started to stare into my eyes. She had a gentler energy about her, and it didn't feel so intrusive when she started probing through my mind. There were images appearing in my mind which showed great destruction and environmental disasters. It was horrible. It was like the Earth was being torn apart. Tears were flooding down my cheeks just seeing the destruction. It was like my emotions were a lot more accentuated and easily manipulated. She suddenly stopped and smiled an almost benevolent smile. She said "Wait here. We're almost done", and with that she walked out.

"After a brief moment two stirrups rose up from either side of the chair. Then something strange started happening. I started feeling really aroused. It was a bit embarrassing as I was alone in a room, but

I was starting to feel really sexually aroused. Very aroused! Then two guys in jumpsuits came in. The jumpsuits were white but there was a hexagonal pattern running through the fabric in a very light grey colour. They seemed like doctors. They gently put my legs into the stirrups. I started to panic; I didn't really want this. I started to writhe, trying to get off the chair, but one of the doctors put his hand just over my forehead and I started to relax and felt much calmer. This now felt natural.

"The doctor moved between my legs and pushed a small device into me. It only seemed small, probably palm sized and rounded and I could feel a coolness pervade my lower body. He then removed the device and told me to "take it easy, this is very precious". I didn't really understand or try to, I just wanted to get out. The chair lurched slightly and moved me into a more upright position. One of the doctors helped me off the chair.

"They led me back to the two women who were waiting in a corridor. The woman motioned me in a direction and told me they would take me home. Next thing I know I am back in my house. I stood there, just getting a sense of my surroundings and I immediately threw up. Virtually projectile vomiting. I make my way to the bathroom and continue to throw up. Despite it being quite early, and abandoning my plans to go out, I decided to go to bed as I was now feeling feverish. My husband soon came home and dealt with the kids, once they came home from school. I spent the evening and night tossing and turning in bed with a fever.

"When I awoke, which was very early for me, I ran to the toilet and threw up. This was different. I'd felt this before. This felt like pregnancy. Once the sickness subsided, the horror of my potential situation became very evident. How could I tell my husband I was pregnant? We weren't really trying for another child, and I felt at the time, me saying it was just a happy accident wouldn't really work. My husband really felt 'something' was going on. I decided best to ignore it as I had no other options. But it was a constant worry in the back of my mind.

"The sickness subsided a few days later so I claimed it was food poisoning. Things generally settled down for a few weeks, aside from the occasional incident with electrical items starting to act-up. Then one Monday afternoon, things started to feel weird, it was a sensation that started to creep up on me. I just got a sense that something wasn't right. Then the two women who visited me last time appeared in the room. At first, they seemed a little perplexed to be there, you could almost see them thinking 'why are we here?'. Then as soon as they saw me, they quickly approached me, as if they suddenly understood what they had to do. I tensed up and one of them grabbed me hard by the arm.

"Next thing I know I am in what looks like an operating theatre but there are very few pieces of equipment. There is a freestanding tower which is coloured gun-metal grey and there is a strip of blue lights towards the top. The lights occasionally pulse. There is a slight hum in the background. The two women are there, the two doctors and there is a small creature in the background. He is about 4 feet tall with an outsized head and large black eyes. I really don't like the look of it. It looks so emotionless.

"The doctors move into position, and they seem to be examining me between my legs. I can't feel them, but I know they are there. They seem to be using this small device again to extract something. They are really concentrating. They are really focussed. Then they straighten up and walk over to the emotionless creature and hand him the device. The creature takes it and leaves the room. The doctors seem relieved and relax a little. They then tell me I have done a great thing. I ask what have I done. I am getting really angry at this point. They say they can't tell me but in the future, everything will become clear to everyone. I start to feel sleepy, and I black out.

"I find myself back in the house. The woman helped me into bed as I was exhausted. I hear them walk downstairs and let themselves out of the front door. I hear it close behind them and I pass out.

"How long I was asleep for I am still unsure of, but I seemed to be asleep for what felt like a long time and awoke to find some blood on the bed sheets. I clean myself up and try to get back into the routine I normally have. The kids come home, often with my husband, and I cook tea, and everything is as it should be. That's what I want, just some normality, but they are all running late it seems. When they do arrive, I can sense that something has happened. They come in the door, and they seem a little dazed, a little like they are not quite with it. My husband starts to explain that as they got near the house there was a grey disc shaped object hovering over the road. He went on to explain that he seemed really drowsy upon seeing the craft then when he 'came to' he was driving down a lane further away from where he saw the craft and about 30 minutes of time was now missing. It was at this point I snapped. I totally lost the plot. It was one thing these beings intruding on my life, but impacting on my children was too much. So, I feel I had a bit of a breakdown at that point.

"I had no way to process these experiences. I can't imagine anyone does. I had no point of reference to manage all this information. So, I just freaked out. I cried for days. Screamed often. And no-one could really help me. No-one understands. No-one can guide you.

"The experiences, I believe, are not happening to my husband but I think they are more interested in myself and the children. As I approach middle-age the experiences seem to involve my children and I have some vague memories of experiences which include my children being on-board craft as well. The experiences continued to have a gynaecological nature for me. I went from having a regular menstrual cycle to having periods that lasted for weeks or I would have a short period every week. It was so physically draining and mentally exhausting.

"My experiences are definitely ongoing and as I age, my experiences seem to change. I expect that I will reach a certain point that they will have no use for me and by then my children will be the centre of their attention. I am just waiting to see more of the tell-tale signs that things are happening to my children and at least I can offer some support, because that is all I can offer. There are too few answers at this point. I can hopefully give them as much normality to counterbalance the strangeness."

9 CASE STUDY #4 - NIKA

Nika is a 53-year-old New Yorker who has been living in London since she relocated there due, in part, to a psychic quest instigated by her early abduction encounters. Nika is of Native American heritage and her discovery of her ancestral roots made an impact in her interaction with the abduction phenomena.

"My grandfather was plagued by what were, I suspect, abduction experiences. He would let little things slip from time to time. He would complain about bad dreams and would claim these bad dreams were from a 'far, distant side of the family'. By family I assumed he meant in a spiritual sense. In later life he would explain that this distant 'star family' were coming back to rediscover something that was buried in our human souls. Everyone thought he was nuts. It was just crazy Native American Grandpa again with his stories! But there is a backstory to where this all started to come to prominence in his and ultimately my life.

I grew up close to New York in a lower middle-class family. The work ethic was drummed into us from an early age. My parents didn't want to see us doing nothing with our day, so play was organised, and if we were at a loose end then chores would be found to keep us busy. So, my sister and I learnt to get up and get out of the house and go play with the other kids to avoid the drudgery of housework.

"As I grew older, I noticed I was different, or at least I felt I was different. I looked physically like everyone else, but I felt different. I felt I was in disguise. I felt, even at that early age, like I was on an undercover mission, just observing what was going on, hiding out being human, I felt like I was undercover waiting for activation. I felt I was waiting for my orders from some secret organisation, which would make everything in my life make some sort of sense. On reflection it was a strange notion for a young kid to have rolling around in their head.

"As I grew into my teens I started to feel really alienated, no pun intended. Alienated and angry. I just didn't get why everyone didn't see the world as I saw it. Why were things the way they were? Why wasn't anyone changing it? I think I was picking up on a lot of injustices I saw and couldn't understand why no-one was doing anything to change these situations. I was idealistic, I guess. In New York you are never far from some real poverty, and that was something I could never understand. In a country with such wealth, why did so many have to go without? In later life my grandfather would remind me that 'There is never peace on stolen land'. Whether that is true or not, I still couldn't understand why there was no-one trying to fix the things that evidently could be fixed.

"In my teens and my early twenties, my encounters would escalate to a point where I felt I was living two lives. My earth life and my life with aliens. Although I rarely used the word or considered them aliens. They were just the 'Others'. They were from elsewhere; they were different in so many ways.

"I have no memories of experiences in my early years, but around 12 years of age I had my first really conscious encounter. I went to bed early, which was unusual on a summer night. We weren't in school, so every day was like a whole holiday in itself. I had this awful headache. It was like someone was trying to crush my head. There was this weird pressure as if there was a tight band around my head. My parents gave me some painkillers and sent me off to bed. The pain was too intense to sleep.

"I lay there tossing and turning, waiting for someone to turn off the pain. Around 11pm I became aware of a dull red light which seemed to be filtering in through a crack in the curtains. I crept to the window to take a look. I was expecting to maybe see a police car or something, but it was a diffuse red light, just floating in the street. I was so puzzled by this, I needed to investigate but couldn't risk going downstairs. I opened the window and became aware of a soft humming sound. Almost like an electricity generator but a bit softer and deeper. There was almost a soothing quality to the sound.

"Suddenly there were two figures in the street. They just appeared from nowhere. They were short, around four feet tall and were looking up at me in the window. They had big, dark eyes, almost the same shape as a cat. Every time our eyes met it was like they were in my head. Almost like we made a connection by looking at each other. Suddenly one of them is standing next to me in the bedroom. I am shocked and stagger back, but he projects into my mind that everything would be ok and that I should feel calm. After he said that, I did feel much calmer. A feeling of almost being relieved swept over me. The next thing I know we are floating together into the light of this red object. It became hazy for a few seconds, and we seemed to be in a larger ship. We drifted along this circular corridor which led us to a room with a large table in it. I was floated onto the table, and I suddenly felt very heavy. It was like I had become heavier somehow and couldn't move. I was becoming a little panicked by this turn of events but again this being just reminded me that nothing bad would happen and I instantly felt calm.

"Another being walked up to the table. I hadn't seen him arrive. He gently lowered his face close to mine. He stared into my eyes, and I became aware of such peace and contentment, but I was aware that he was looking for something inside my head. Almost as if he was waiting for a memory or thought to present itself to him. I say him, as he felt male to me. There was nothing to indicate gender other than what I felt. Suddenly he stopped and pulled back. He seemed really happy with what had happened. It's what I sensed. Suddenly, in my head, he simply said "Good". I felt the weight ease and I was floated off the table. The atmosphere suddenly changed. I felt everything seem really efficient. They wanted me gone now. They had achieved whatever it was they wanted, and now I must go. I suddenly found myself in the street in front of this light. The original being was there, we both then appeared in my bedroom, he said to me telepathically 'We will maintain. We will return.' I didn't really understand the statement in total, but I started feeling sleepy and crawled into bed. The moment I got into bed, the headache ceased, just like someone switching off a light. Gone!

"This occurred eight or nine times over the next year in an identical fashion. The headache followed by the encounter. Towards the end these encounters become so typical to me. It was just what happened. The headache would come, and I knew what was going to follow.

"As I grew older, I started to notice other humans on the ship. I would start to be taken into larger rooms, still for examinations, but there were others there too. I started to detect the stress in the air. Some people were really freaking out, or there would be others looking almost traumatised. The aliens though, were quick to deal with anyone losing control or slowing down whatever was meant to happen. I started to notice, over time, that there would be familiar faces. Almost like we were a batch of humans all being taken at the same time. Maybe there's a rota? Maybe we were all part of the same study group?

"As I started to develop sexually, maybe around 17 years of age onwards, the aliens took a greater notice in my reproductive system. When I had an experience, my periods would go haywire for a few months afterwards. When nature balanced herself out, the aliens would arrive again and start poking around. During these experiences they seemed fascinated with my, shall we say, inner workings?

"Anyway, sometimes during these examinations of my vagina one of the taller Greys would look into my eyes and it was almost as if he was manipulating me to feel deep maternal feelings. It became a battle of wills, which ultimately, I would lose, but I didn't want to think about that maternal side of me. Those feelings weren't real. I didn't feel ready. I also felt that I would be the one to decide when I felt maternal, not them. I didn't want them poking and prodding and playing with my mind. It had gone too far for me. I guess I started to act up not only during the encounters but in life as well. I had dropped out of school, I was just this ball of anger and I was not happy with myself or anyone at that time. I was so angry.

"Things then took a bit of a turn. The unspoken but open secret in my family was that there was some Native American blood in the family tree. It was a secret inasmuch it wasn't spoken about, there was no story, there was no shame, it just came up in conversation from time to time at family gatherings but as a topic of conversation it was shut down pretty quickly by my family. I think they had collectively worked hard to get to a comfortable existence and there was some compromise there, which no-one was keen to acknowledge or unpick. The compromise being, in retrospect, playing capitalism's game and turning their back on other ideas. Maybe.

"Then one day my grandfather came to me and told of an experience that occurred to him, which brought the Native American ideas and traditions back to the forefront for me. My grandfather told me that he had worked hard all his life in construction and knew some of the old stories from the 'old ways', but at the time it was better to fit in with his surroundings and not rock the boat. But as he got older, he kept having these experiences with what we would call Greys. They plagued him to a degree because he couldn't contextualise these experiences into the world view which he and many others had. It just didn't fit.

"So, my grandfather decided to go back to the old ways, as he described it. He spent a bit of time looking into doing a sweat lodge to see if he could get some resolution in regard to the encounters he was having. Through a friend of a friend type connection, my grandfather travelled into New York State and underwent his first sweat lodge. He recounted to me how he felt a great weight lift off his shoulders, as if by simply acknowledging his ancestors in this way, there was some psychic energy being directed his way. My grandfather apparently went into a trance and received a lot of messages explaining that even by ignoring his ancestry he couldn't remove what was in his blood. This was part of him whether he chose to ignore it, or not.

"He was apparently also told that the Greys he had been encountering, he didn't use the word Greys, but that's who he was talking about, had always been here and just like people there were good and bad. The message he took away for me was that I was to always vision quest after my encounters, that would give me some insight and ground me back on planet Earth in an energetic sense, but it would also provide me with answers.

"When I was originally told this, I was sceptical, although relieved that I wasn't the only person having these alien encounters. I didn't know really what a vision quest was and how it would ever help. I lived in New York City; I never saw many vision questers there. Is that a sign your neighbourhood is becoming more gentrified? Joggers and vision questers, that must mean my house is worth more! After his experience at the sweat lodge, my grandfather changed. He was always a hard drinking, out with the boys, brash New York guy. But suddenly he became much more thoughtful, he began researching his Native American beliefs, he stopped drinking, he really slowed his pace of life and his personal energy right down. He became much more philosophical. That is the profoundness that such encounters with something larger than ourselves can be. That's not to say these encounters were 'good'. I think you learn more from bad experiences.

"I sat with 'my message' for a good few months, maybe 6 to 9 months, until a particularly tough encounter forced me to decide that I wasn't going to be such a passive participant in these experiences.

"I was in my early twenties when this encounter happened. I sat on the porch of my mother's house, just watching the day go by with a coffee. Something kept catching the sun and reflecting in my eyes. I kept looking around expecting to see some kid messing with a mirror or something, but I couldn't see where this was coming from. Then I became aware of a low bass-type rumble, which was so low it felt like it was vibrating into my body. The hairs on my arms were prickling up. I could feel this vibration in my chest and inner ear. Then suddenly two beings appeared at the end of the path to the house and motioned for me to follow. As I took a step towards them a slit of white light appeared and expanded wide enough for us to enter. It was if someone was opening a curtain for us, from this reality to another. When we stepped through, we were on a craft, all shiny walls and surfaces. It made no sense, but it sort of did. All the weirdness of life is just a breath away from us. It exists alongside us, I feel.

"So, after a short walk down a corridor I am led into a room with the familiar examination table on. I hop up with no instruction and lie back. They're fumbling with my clothes, and I am soon naked. A taller Grey steps into my line of vision and starts looking deep into my eyes and slowly I am becoming turned-on. Part of me is raging again because it's like he has a button he can press and it's all so easy. Then one of the Greys moves between my legs and he has a long, thin silver device which he starts to insert into my vagina. It's a bit uncomfortable but I wasn't resisting too much. There is a slight vibrating sensation once it's inserted. Then as the process finishes, and everyone seems happy, I get off the table and dress myself.

"I am led past a few closed doorways and then I am led into a room where there is a chair that seems to be joined to the floor so it looks like a big chair shaped blob just pushed through the floor. On the wall in front of the chair is a large screen. I sit in the chair which feels like it is made of a hard plastic and it feels like it is vibrating ever so slightly. The screen flickers on and it looks like a nature documentary which occasionally cuts to scenes of natural disasters. Then there are images of me naked, and images of me having sex on the ship with a total stranger! So now I freak out! Is this what is going to happen? Are they going to make it happen! When do I get a say in all this? Can we stop this happening? Why am I being shown this?

"The images stop, and I am led to the corridor, and I am seething. I go back the same way I arrived, a doorway opens up and I am back on the street, but it is much later. As soon as I take a few steps something inside me tells me I am pregnant. I just know it. I just feel it. I walked into the house, my parents assuming I went for a walk somewhere. I am trying to hold it together because my mind is racing with all those images I saw and the thought that I could be pregnant. How dare they? I am a sovereign being! Who do they think they are?

"I make my excuses and head for my room. I am lurching between rage and practicality. I'm angry but still trying to fathom out what I am going to do next. How do I explain this? Space aliens made me pregnant was never going to be a phrase I wanted to utter. Eventually, totally exhausted, I fell asleep. When I slept, I had this dream. In the dream there was a Grey telling me that everything was going to be ok, and I wasn't to do anything, they would take care of everything. It was repeated over and over through the dream, just so I understood the message. I say this felt like a dream, but it might have been some sort of telepathic message.

"I woke late that morning. I was really confused. It felt all so unreal. I spent the next few days in a bit of a mental fog. I felt totally bewildered and I really felt as if I had nowhere to turn. Then I was hit by the message my grandfather gave me. I can get an answer to this, I thought, there is a way forward. I would go on a vision quest. I did some quick research on how to do this. I had a friend who was a bit New Age and a bit of an old hippy, and he explained the basics.

"I felt stupid to start with, but I walked. I left my mother's house and just walked. I tried to look for signs, guidance, or synchronicity to guide me. Exhausted after four hours of continual walking I headed home thoroughly fed up and dejected. I had seen so much of my neighbourhood and beyond, but no great answer. No divine light showing me the way. I changed into a nightdress thinking that I would get comfortable and sleep for a while. As I led there, I could feel something in my lower abdomen. It felt like a dead weight was suddenly being applied there. Something felt wrong down there. Something was pushing down inside me. I had never felt anything like this before and I felt like something was happening that shouldn't be happening.

"A few moments later there was a pure white glow starting to emanate from the end of my bed. There were two Greys now standing at the end of my bed. I just knew this was connected with my vision quest and what was happening in my body. Next thing I am aware of I am on a table with the taller Grey looking into my eyes. He seemed concerned. That is what it felt like. It was as if he was trying to find out what had happened recently. The smaller Greys are back between my legs, and they have another long silver, cylindrical object, identical to the same one they had used previously. It's gone inside me, and it is quite painful. I feel a hand on my head and the pain starts to fade away. The tall Grey simply tells me that I wasn't ready for this, and he leaves. I assume he is referring to whatever they were trying to achieve between my legs. I find myself back home. My nightdress has been clumsily replaced. About an hour seemed to have passed. I sleep but am awoken by very painful menstrual cramps. I had very heavy bleeding for about 7 days. It was extremely unpleasant. It was almost as if I had miscarried.

"Things were quiet for a couple of weeks. I nervously felt that things were returning to normality. But I now really felt I was involved with something way beyond my full understanding and my control. I decided I really needed some spiritual intervention or something that I could utilise to help me understand these experiences. So, I leaned heavily into this concept of vision questing as I felt that I could access the realms that these beings were coming from or operating in.

"I decided to get out of the city and start working on myself and try to understand what situation I was now ensnared in. I rented a cabin for a week and decided I was going to try and meet these entities halfway rather than them always calling the shots. I got to the cabin with my supplies for the week and I decided I would use the local hiking trails for my vision quest. That was my plan. I thought it was foolproof. I used the first day just to get an idea of the locality. It all felt really normal, and I felt such a fool for trying to do this, but there was also something really deep within me that was now awakening.

"I got up early on the second day and meditated for a short while. I then headed out. It was a glorious morning. I had been walking for an hour and slowly I got the feeling I was being followed. I tried to shake the feeling off, thinking my mind was playing tricks on me. I was walking through a slightly wooded area, and I suddenly started to hear an electrical crackling in the air. I turned to see a bright red light moving through the trees. The centre of the light was so bright it was painful to look at for too long. It was gently moving through the trees in my direction. The light suddenly moved very quickly and positioned itself in the pathway in front of me. Suddenly the small light grew in size and started to gently pulse. I could almost feel an electrical tingle on my skin as it pulsed. I closed my eyes and suddenly all these images were flashing through my mind. Images from my early life. Images I didn't recognise or understand. I saw images of London repeatedly. I didn't understand why at the time as I had no connection to the place. I opened my eyes and found myself on a craft. They had snatched me from that hiking trail.

"There were two Greys who took me by the hands and led me to a large room where there was a taller Grey. They led me to this very cold, metallic table. They told me, telepathically, to get onto the table. I led on the table and suddenly there was a force pinning me down. I tried to talk to them, but I just couldn't get the words out. The larger Grey had this very long needle in his hand. He then inserted the needle up my left nostril. He pushed it really far. I could feel it pushing right up into my nose cavity. It felt as if it was pushing up into my brain. Suddenly it was retracted, and the larger Grey lent over my face and he started staring deep into my eyes. It was almost as if he was making some sort of connection. It was almost as if he was activating or tuning in to whatever was put up my nose. The larger

Grey straightened up and looked at the other Greys as if he was communicating with them and then turned and left.

"The two Greys helped me off the table and led me deeper into the craft. We moved into a larger room which had all these large tubes which seemed to connect to the floor and ceiling. Inside these tubes was a blue solution and in the solution were these human bodies just floating in the liquid. I was terrified. These bodies seemed lifeless just floating in the liquid. Just suspended and floating aimlessly. I asked what this was about, but I received no answer. They looked dead. What happened to them? I know what I saw.

"I was then led into another room where there were several rows of what I can only describe as baby incubators. In these incubators were these very strange looking babies. All these babies seemed so listless. None of them moved. The two Greys motioned to me to get closer to the babies, but I felt really repulsed. There was something strange about them. I couldn't do what they wanted me to, despite their insistence.

"As I was standing there, I started to get these images flashing into my mind. Images of me holding these babies. I got feelings of a bond forming between us. It was repulsive to me as I didn't feel connected to them. I turned away and the Greys seemed disappointed in me. They led me away and back to the corridor.

"I suddenly found myself back on the wooded trail and I suddenly had this sharp pain in the back of my head. I felt something wet under my nostril and noticed my nose was bleeding. I headed back to the cabin as I was starting to get really tired. When I got back, I collapsed into bed and slept. I dreamt about what had happened on the ship, and these babies and also about London. None of this made sense. How could it make sense?

"I got up after sleeping and decided to try vision questing to get some answers. I walked the same trail again and as soon as I got to the same wooded area, I had this acute pain in my abdomen and the pain returned to the back of my head. I was doubled in pain. It was horrendous. I couldn't move. This guy appeared on the track ahead of me. He came and asked if I was ok. I was breathless with the pain. I managed to say where my cabin was, and he started to help me along the track towards my cabin. As we walked the guy explained he was re-walking this trail as he had seen this UFO the day before. He joked about not being crazy and I stopped in my tracks. He explained that he had seen this grey disc hovering above the wooded area, then he said he saw it morph into a small red orb. I explained that I had seen the red orb moving through the trees. I didn't tell him the full story as I didn't want him to think I was crazy. He said he had returned hoping to see it again. This helped me feel a little more sane that someone had also seen the same object that had taken me.

"We got back to the cabin, and I thanked him for helping me. He was concerned about me, but the pain was starting to subside. I offered him a coffee and as we drank coffee, he explained that he had seen a lot of craft in his time. He suddenly seemed very sheepish and said that I would probably think him crazy, but he has been taken by aliens several times. He said that these craft seem to follow him everywhere. There was a pause where I suspected he thought I would start laughing or make some joke of it. I just said to him that the craft he saw had taken me.

"At first, I thought he would think I was teasing him, but I explained my journey and he seemed to understand. We spent the rest of the day comparing notes. He had seemed to have had a wide range of experiences with the Greys. Then all of a sudden, I realised the guy sitting in front of me, the guy I am happily chatting to in my cabin, is the guy I saw myself having sex with in my earlier experiences. I had to play it cool as firstly I didn't want to give this guy the wrong idea plus I didn't want him to think I was totally weird.

"But this highlights how the Greys are constantly manipulating your entire life. The places you end up, the situations you find yourself in, the people you meet, it is as if you are some sort of proxy for them. With that knowledge, you become suspicious of people who come into your life, or those weird, little synchronicities, because you start to think 'Oh, is this for me, or has this been orchestrated for them?' and the worst thing is, you'll never know.

"Anyway, I had this chat with this mystery guy (Gary) and it was kind of satisfying to have this type of discussion, because most people who have these experiences often have periods of isolation as they can't really discuss these things with most people. So, after a discussion with Gary about our experiences he went on his way back to where he was staying.

"The evening was drawing in so I decided on an early night. I locked the cabin up, spent some time meditating and I drifted to sleep. I was awoken a few hours later by this piercing white light shining into the bedroom. I could see this orb of white light, almost like an eye, peeping in the gap between the curtain and the window frame. It kept moving, changing its position outside the window, almost like it was looking for me or as if it was trying to get a better position to see me. The room was soon bathed in this intense light that seemed to be emanating from the window. These two beings started to walk out of the light into the room and made their way to the bed. They took both my arms and led me into the light. Just like walking from one room into another I was on the ship.

"I am led to an examination room and a taller Grey comes into the room. It has the Doctor/Orchestrator vibe to it. Then in comes Gary, totally naked and very aroused, but he looks like he is in a trance. He is not acknowledging me or his surroundings. Then another woman, who I haven't seen before comes into the room. She is also naked and also seems in a total trance. The Doctor Grey looks at me for a while and then goes and stares into the eyes of the other woman. As if being telepathically commanded to, the other woman goes over to Gary and starts kissing and caressing him, and then nature takes its course! They are having sex on this slab that appears to be moulded to the wall. The Doctor then leads me into the corridor and into another room. We are behind a glass wall, and on the other side of the glass wall are several children, of varying ages. They seem to be engaged in play and learning. The Doctor communicates to me, telepathically, that these are all Gary's children that he has produced for them. These are the children of the future, the Doctor states. The Doctor states that I need to be involved in building a future for humanity. I don't really understand the full implications of that statement but reading between the lines I felt that this was some breeding program, but I have no clue as to what the future entails that would require a breeding program.

"I feel really confused and The Doctor leads me back to the corridor and then the other two Greys lead me down the corridor and I find myself back in the cabin, alone.

"I felt exhausted and crawled into bed, then had a series of vivid dreams. I use the word dreams, but it felt to me that this information had been downloaded to me on previous encounters and now was the time for it to be revealed. The images were apocalyptic, but it was not Earth. It was somewhere in deep space. A civilisation was destroying itself. Then there were images, on this planet, of environmental disaster, weird weather and many people dying as a result. I could understand the parallels. I woke very early in the morning and decided to get out and try to vision quest for some sort of answer. I packed a bag, some water and decided to go where I felt moved to go.

"I moved from trail to trail, with no plan. The further I walked the more I seemed to unlock more feelings on how I felt about this whole situation I was in and what to do next. I kept seeing the apocalyptic images and I felt they were trying to remind me that I had to help in some way. As if people who were being taken were part of some program or plan. By the end of my vision quest, I felt a sense of being more grounded. I felt that I had a path to follow, but unsure of these entities. Almost as if I had to walk this path irrespective of who I encountered and their objectives. I had to be true to me and my journey as a first priority and deal with whatever I encountered as a second priority. I decided I had all the information I could from this trip and planned to leave the next day.

"I returned to my cabin and packed, ready for an early exit. I was tidying a few things when there was a knock at the door. It was Gary. He looked really tired and drawn. He said that I wasn't going to believe this, but he felt he had an experience last night. I told him I knew. I told him I was there and witnessed the whole thing. This totally blew his mind. He couldn't remember much of the actual experience, so I filled in the blanks for him. He looked totally shocked, but he felt it tied in with his knowledge of previous encounters he had experienced.

"Then a heavy silence settled. Where do you go from there? How do you deal with such information? It is a feeling most experiencers have to deal with. He decided to return to his cabin. I felt a little unnerved for some reason, so I didn't tell him of my intentions to leave early. I felt I was on a mission now and I didn't really know who I could trust, especially considering how people seemed to be easily manipulated by these entities.

"I drove back to my parents' house the following morning, getting away just as the day was breaking. It felt good to be moving away from that heaviness of the last few days. I got back to find a letter waiting for me. I had been in and out of jobs, mainly due to my inability to focus on the normal stuff of life, and to my parents' consternation I hadn't really developed a career for myself. I had applied for this job in New York City, and I had been offered that job. It was working in the research industry and to my parents it seemed like a real profession. The company I would be working for conducted research on a variety of subjects for large multinational companies. It seemed really interesting and varied, which suited me as I got bored doing the same thing, constantly. In the letter was something that hadn't been mentioned in the job advert or in the interview; there were regular secondments to London. The penny dropped. All those images of London now made sense. Whether these images were planted there by the Greys or whether I somehow psychically picked up on something I am still unsure, but the reason why London was in my mind now was clear. This was part of my mission.

"I had to do a few months in New York before they trusted me enough to send me to London. During this time my experiences seemed to stop. The work was pretty full-on with a steep learning curve. Maybe they left me alone, who knows? They definitely seemed to be absent. Anyway, I took the plane to London for my week-long trip. I checked into my hotel and felt like I needed to sleep. After a quick shower I slipped into bed and tried to sleep. There was something making me feel unsettled. A feeling. A vibration. I just couldn't settle. Then I noticed a light emanating from underneath the bathroom door. The light was pulsing to a very subtle bass-like rhythm. It sounded ominous. It sounded really foreboding. I was scared by it. I tried to get out of bed, but my legs felt like lead. I could barely move. The light seemed to be seeping around all the edges of the door. The door started to slowly open, and the light flooded into the room. Then I found myself on an examination bed on a craft. The lights were so bright it was difficult to see. The light seemed to be coming from everywhere and not just one light source. It was as if the whole craft was emitting light. There were four smaller Greys standing around the examination table and a taller Grey at the head of the table, looking down at me. He was staring into my eyes, and I was feeling very emotional. They were making me feel very emotional. An examination of my body started. They prodded everywhere and then the taller Grey produced what looked like a clear wand that emanated light. At the tip was a very intense white light. The taller Grey moved around so he was now at my side and then gently, at first inserted the wand up my nose and then slowly pushed it deep into my skull. There was a moment of intense pain then it was retracted. The taller Grey then started to start deep into my eyes. It felt like he was searching for something. Memories, most of them long forgotten and seemingly random, appeared in my mind. It was like watching a movie of these random scenes from my past.

"I suddenly felt very cold hands pushing my legs apart. I could do nothing to prevent it, my legs felt so heavy. Then another tall Grey approached with a faintly glowing cylindrical device. It was only a few inches long and glowed with a slight sparkly nature. I felt it being slowly pushed into me. The taller Grey started staring into my eyes and started evoking a lot of sexual memories, some from my past and many I didn't really recognise. Although I didn't recognise some of the images, I seemed to be involved in them. I couldn't help being really turned on by these images which were being implanted in my memory. I felt I was getting close to orgasm. Which partly infuriated me as none of this was consensual, but I just didn't have the mental power to break out of what was happening to me. Suddenly, the mental images stopped, and the tall Greys stepped away. As usual, they appeared or felt to me, very happy with themselves. I don't understand why.

"I felt back in control of my legs, and I was helped off the table by the smaller Greys and they escorted me through the corridors to this mezzanine level which looked over a very large room. In that room were many examination tables where a lot of women and men were being examined by taller Greys. Moving between the tables were smaller Greys who usually seem to be in a supporting or helper role. One of the smaller Greys turned to me and spoke to me, telepathically. 'You must now start to help them, as your time is short'. I didn't really understand, and he picked up on that confusion and said, 'We must find your way to the Source'. He quickly turned me around, obviously not wanting to explain more, and started to escort me back through the corridor. I suddenly found myself in my room, just standing there feeling a little tired. I crawled back into bed and fell asleep.

"I awoke and felt like shit. I had to pull myself together and get into my work frame of mind, however, I felt different. I felt slightly less like myself. I felt as if I had changed somehow but couldn't explain why. I showered, downed some coffee, and made my way to the office I was working from. A typical day ensued, and I was happy when 5pm came. I got back to the hotel and decided, after a shower, to get a bit of a walk and see if I could understand what had happened to me last night.

"I showered, changed, had a quick snack, and headed out. I had been walking for a while when I came to a street crossing. As I waited, I saw a woman who kept looking at me. I smiled and she returned the smile. Then she said, "I know you'll think this is crazy, but it is like I know you somehow. I think you need to start sharing your experiences and you need to help others come to a realisation about what is actually going on.". I knew exactly what she meant, and I said, which was totally out of character for me, "Let's get a coffee and discuss."

"We went to a nearby coffee shop, and she unburdened her life story of being an abductee. She felt that she had been used as a breeder for these hybridised children for the last ten years. We traded a lot of stories and I realised that this was just like me meeting Gary. People were coming to me to give me some guidance and tell me their stories. These stories were helping me to build a larger picture of what was happening with the abduction phenomena. I doubt anyone will ever be able to explain the whole abduction phenomena as it has not only been ongoing for a long time, but it is always slowly adapting. Changing as required.

"After our discussion, we swapped details and arranged to keep in touch. By the time I got back to the hotel, I was really excited. The vision questing had paid off for me. Embracing the phenomena, for me, helped me to move forward in my limited understanding. There is a large part of me that thinks that you can interact with this phenomena, but the Greys will always have an upper hand because they understand the realms they operate in better than any human ever will. But by not being totally passive, I was learning more about them and myself.

"I got back to New York to find my employer was absolutely over the moon with my performance in the London office. I was going to be travelling to London a lot more frequently. I felt this was all part of some cosmic masterplan. A few weeks of normality followed but I felt that there was something inside of me. It just didn't feel comfortable down there. Was that object still in me? I decided to find out. I called my doctor and asked if I could schedule a scan. I had to be very vague as I couldn't reveal the whole story behind why I needed a scan. The scan was arranged for the following day as someone had cancelled their appointment, opening up the schedule for me. I turned up, very excited to see if something was inside me and to get some proof that this was really as I was experiencing it. I got to the doctor and as soon as I got into the examination room, the entire building was hit by a power cut. The power was out only for that building on the block. The staff were perplexed but it didn't surprise me at all. The Greys were obviously not going to allow this scan to happen.

"I left the Doctor's office having re-booked the exam, but deep down I knew this scan would not be allowed to take place. Later that night I had an experience where the Greys retrieved a small metallic object from inside me. I was in bed, relaxing at home when the power cut and I just knew that they were coming back for me. There was static electricity in the air. I sat up and listened. I couldn't hear anything, there were no real hints to their presence other than the lack of power and the occasional feeling of static. Then suddenly, just as if someone had flicked a switch, three small Greys were standing around my bed. Then I blacked out. I came around on a craft. The lights were really dim, almost dark. The air was musty and stale. I was led into a room and helped onto a bed. There was a sudden invisible pressure pushing down on me. I couldn't move. I looked toward the door and saw two large Greys come in and position themselves at the foot of the bed.

"Two stirrup type attachments extended out of the bed and my legs were placed onto them. At this point, I couldn't really feel my body. I blacked out for a short while and came around to see the larger Greys walking out of the room with a small, dimly glowing, grey, metallic object on a tray. They had removed the object. I blacked out again and came round back in my room. I felt empty, and I felt as if something had been stolen from me. Whatever the object that had been inside me, it was highly prized by the Greys that they couldn't let my doctor discover its existence. It is always this game of cat and mouse with the Greys.

"Again, after that experience, once I had rested a little, I went back to vision questing to make sense of it all. I have started using more ritual work connected with my Native American background in conjunction with the vision questing. All that inner and outer work will help me, but it doesn't stop the encounters, it doesn't stop the trauma of the experiences, but it seems to help me move through them easier.

"Since that first trip to London, people were always being sent my way, for want of a better phrase, and were unburdening themselves in regard to their experiences. It is almost like I am helping bring these memories out of people. I am almost like a Dula to a lot of experiencers. I seem to unlock a lot of meaning to their experiences as well as unlocking memories. I really believe that if experiencers try to confront or challenge their passive nature towards the phenomena, they can get a better understanding and can sometimes find some meaning within their experiences. The frightening part of this is the huge number of people having these experiences. It is not just a few people, it is a lot of people. Which then points to the huge scale of whatever is going with these experiences. Plus this has been going on for decades! We know so little and we are permitted to know so little. That is the scary part for me: just what is going on that we don't know about?"

Nika continues to work with abductees/experiencers on a casual basis, helping them come to terms with their experiences. Nika continues to have regular experiences herself.

10 CASE STUDY #5 - JANA

Jana has been having abduction experiences since her teenage years. Jana has been moving through a variety of support groups to try and find some reason for her ongoing experiences. Often feeling alone and vulnerable due to these experiences, Jana has suffered for many years trying to find the 'why' in these experiences.

"I grew up in a working-class environment and I felt this anchored me for a long time. I knew where I was literally and metaphorically. Then one day, all that changed. Everything I took for granted, everything I thought I knew, in fact just about everything was now turned upside down. It started with a little bright light, somewhere off in the distance as I walked home from school. It was the winter, so it was getting dark in the evenings very quickly. I had stopped off at a friend's house after school and I was now walking the short distance to my house. As I climbed the hill towards my house I noticed a pinpoint of light on the horizon. It was a grey and cloudy evening, and the darkness of night was fast approaching. This pinpoint of light suddenly arced towards me and hovered above my head, maybe about 200 feet above. It was glowing so bright it was illuminating the clouds above it. It was painful to look at but I couldn't take my eyes off it.

"The glow started to dim slightly, and I could see that it looked like a grey flat circle. Suddenly a beam of light, just like a spotlight, shot out from under the object and was now shining down on me. I tried to continue walking as I was really scared now but my feet were rooted to the spot. I just couldn't get my legs to move. Suddenly I was moving up towards the object. I could see my view change as I was pulled up toward the object. I don't remember actually passing into the craft, but I suddenly found myself inside the object. I was still in this spotlight so I couldn't really see much around me. From what I could tell, I was in a circular room. Suddenly, from out of the darkness two beings stepped into the light. They were what you would call Greys. They were around four feet tall, with the classic outsized head and large eyes. They just stared for a while. Just looking at me. Totally devoid of emotion. Then they stepped back into the darkness and the spotlight turned off briefly and the room became properly illuminated.

"The room was circular in shape with a very high ceiling which also looked domed. The walls looked like an off-white colour. The temperature was a little on the cool side. It was silent. Almost too silent, as if there was something stopping any noise, like some sort of dampening. The beings turned and walked to a doorway. In my mind, I guess telepathically, they told me to follow them. Which I did. We walked into the corridor and followed it round until we were in what looked like an examination room. In the middle of the room was a rectangular slab, just floating in mid-air. It was the size of a single bed mattress and looked to be made from a very smooth material. It was white coloured, and it was humming. I was asked to get on the bed, but I was a little nervous as I couldn't really see how I could manage it. I was thinking that if I sat on it, it might hit the floor. As I thought that the Greys reassured me, and I hopped on.

"It was like getting on a concrete slab, it felt that hard at first. Then as I settled into a more comfortable position it felt as if it was getting a little softer. Almost as if it was bending to my shape. Every now and again I would start to panic slightly as this was obviously a very unusual position for a 15-year-old schoolgirl to find herself in. Whenever the panic started to set in, I would hear one of their voices tell me to relax, that everything would be fine and that I had nothing to worry about. The voice sounded a little emotionless, with no real accent to speak of. Once they spoke, I did start to relax. Then from the corner of my eye I saw a much taller Grey walk towards me. This one must have been around 5 and a half feet tall. This one was in a white garment, and it all started to feel very medically oriented. In their hand was what looked like a glowing crystal. It was glowing a soft white colour. It was oblong with a point at each end. The taller Grey moved to the end of the slab and moved my feet apart. I could now feel the other Greys clumsily moving my clothes. The one smaller Grey had a dull, metallic looking tube which was being positioned between my legs. I could feel this tube being inserted inside me and it was very painful. The taller Grey moved towards my head and placed the glowing crystal on my forehead, with the pointed end facing towards my nose. Suddenly the pain started to subside and as the pain started to subside, the crystal started to dim slightly.

"The taller Grey returned to their position between my legs. The three Greys were all down there, doing whatever they were doing. Then the taller Grey took the metallic tube and left the room. The other Greys fixed my clothing, and the one Grey removed the crystal, which instantly started glowing a lot brighter. There was a sudden shooting pain between my legs as the crystal was removed. I started to cry with the pain. Then I heard them explain that the pain would subside and that I had been very helpful. I instantly asked, 'How?'. Their response was that now was not the time for questions or explanations. The slab lowered so I could step off and I was led to the centre of the craft. The bright spotlight was switched on and I suddenly found myself back on the street. The object hovered in the sky for a few seconds then shot up at an incredible speed.

"Normally, I would have run home from there, but I was still in some discomfort, so I slowly walked home. The rain was now starting. By the time I got in I was soaked. I looked at the clock in the kitchen and I saw that I was back much later than I should have been. I had lost an hour due to the incident. I made an excuse and went upstairs to get changed. As I got changed into dry clothes, I noticed there was a rash between my legs. It was a light, pink rash and slightly puffy. I knew I couldn't explain this to my parents, so I just got changed and got into the usual rhythm of the house. By the time I went to bed, the rash had faded. I always had great difficulty getting to sleep, but this experience must have exhausted me because I fell asleep immediately.

"The next day I awoke and had a slight throbbing between my legs. It was also a little like period pains also, so I assumed I was getting my period a little early. As I left for school, I was a little anxious. I was expecting them to return again. I felt very vulnerable. Apart from the odd twinge inside me, I was able to move beyond the memory of what happened. Not just the memory but move beyond the thought of what had happened. I suppose I was still numb to what had happened, the implications of which were about to impact my life.

"Anyway, my period became very late. I wasn't sexually active, but I was now concerned that my period was over 3 months late directly after my first experience. It was difficult to broach with my mother, but I explained that my period was late and my mother, who was amazingly pragmatic about such stuff, just explained that things like this happen from time to time. My mother, who I believe in retrospect had her own ET encounters, was basically telling me just to get on with life.

"Around 6 months later my period had gotten back to normal, and I had pushed that experience to the back of my mind. I rarely thought about it. However, I was hanging out with some friends when my next experience happened. We were hanging out at a friend's house, there were four of us in total. We were just listening to some music and chatting. The usual stuff at that age. Suddenly the power went off. I went down with my friend to see if the fuse box had tripped, but it hadn't. Suddenly the power came back on and went off again quickly. It was as if someone was turning the power on and off at random intervals. Suddenly there was a flash of light and everyone except me was frozen in place. They looked like statues.

"I turned to find two Greys standing behind me. Again, speaking directly to my mind they explained I had to follow them. I started to move only to find myself suddenly back in the same craft again. I followed them to the examination room where the same procedure took place. After another painful procedure I was taken to a room where there were women nursing these babies. The babies looked strange. There was something not right about them. They looked human, but there was something that made them not look quite human. The baby's hair was wispy, dark and brittle looking and their eyes seemed to be very dark. They looked dark and as a result seemed void of emotion. I felt at the time there was no life to these weird little children. They seemed very listless. The one Grey spoke to my mind and said "Our species are to become one. We can give you so much and we require so little". Again, I asked what that meant, but again I was met with another vague riddle. "We share your past and we will again share a future with you". The Grey then said that I was helping with their plan, and I should be happy as I will be remembered for my contribution. I came to the conclusion that I would get no straight answers, but I could piece together that I was somehow involved in these weird procedures that were producing these strange children.

"I was led away from the baby room, and I was told that this would be my future from now on. I suddenly found myself back in my friend's house with the electricity continuing to act very weird. My friends were blissfully unaware that anything had happened. I decided to leave as I had to get my head around what exactly was happening to me. Again, another slice of what I now know as missing time. I seemed to have been gone for around 30 minutes. How could people be frozen in place like this? It was all too much, but more troubling was the invasion of my body for unknown purposes. Back then UFOs and aliens were something you didn't confess to being interested or connected with, there was a stigma. People would think you were crazy. So I just had to keep things quiet. After this experience I seemed to be continually on my period. I had period symptoms for at least 6 weeks. It was so difficult to manage. I was just constantly bleeding.

"This process of being taken every few months and going through some sort of gynaecological procedures went on for a few years until I was 23. I was feeling like I was just a piece of meat in someone else's experiment. Plus, it was hard having my menstrual cycle constantly in a state of chaos. There was no-one to talk to. No-one would understand or believe me.

"At 23, the experiences changed somewhat. I would continue to be taken at times to suit their agenda, I couldn't really find any meaningful schedule, it just seemed to be at random intervals, but it was regular enough to remain a presence in my life. But now I was being introduced to these weird, hybrid children. The first time it happened I was sleeping at my parents' house. I was awoken in the early morning by a bright light shining through a gap in the curtains. The light was piercingly bright, so much so I had to shield my eyes to make sense of the scene. I got up out of bed and moved toward the window. There is a grey disc silently hovering above the house, and this intense beam of light is projecting into my room. I look up and down the street. It is the perfect juxtaposition of a normal working-class street at night and the unimaginable technological power of some unknown force. Two totally disconnected worlds that for some reason, I was bridging.

"The light started to get brighter, and I detected a subtle humming noise as the intensity of the light increased. I felt an intense tingling sensation and I felt a little light-headed and found myself in that circular room again. I was led down the now familiar corridor and into a room where there were about a dozen hi-tech looking, well, the best word for them word be incubators. They looked to be made from a clear material. They were shaped like a tic-tac and in each of them was one of these weird looking children, who appeared to be asleep, but lying in a position very unnatural for children. They were all led on their backs with their arms by their sides. They were led out as if you would lie a body in a coffin.

"One of the Greys that was accompanying me moved and opened the lid of one of the incubators. I was told to pick the child up. I did so and it felt a little cool to the touch. I held it as you would hold a baby. For a while I was convinced it was dead as it seemed so motionless. Then it started to open its eyes very slowly. Once the eyes were opened, I found myself locked into some sort of communication. Somehow these children know so much at an early age. Almost as if this has been programmed into them. Or maybe this is some sort of genetic memory, if such a thing exists. But looking into their eyes I got more information than I got from any of the Greys as to what this was all about. It seemed like I had some download of information from that first encounter with the hybrids. Over the next few weeks, that download would unpack itself and I would have realisations as I went about my day-to-day existence.

"My understanding was, and I still believe this, the Greys were a lifeform created for a specific purpose. They are an advanced programmable life form that carries within it all the thoughts, experiences and beliefs of its creators. Whether they have this in themselves or whether they access it like a hive mind, I am unsure, and that is probably irrelevant. They were sent out into the universe to find a new host for their creators to exist in. Hence the perceived hybridisation of humans and this alien life-form. We have the connection to a higher power that the Greys and their creators want. The Greys and their creators believe they can pour themselves into the physical blueprint of a human and access all that humanity has. However, the program isn't working as well as they would like, hence the ongoing project of abducting humans to achieve this hybridisation. Plus, I strongly believe the Greys want these hybrids to live on Earth at some point, but this can only be achieved once the hybrids can function better. There is something fundamentally wrong with them, but what that is I couldn't say as I just don't know. The Greys also believe that humanity will cease to exist in its current form through a variety of events, mainly self-inflicted. The Greys believe they can then inherit the Earth for themselves and their hybrids. I believe that is why they are so fixated, from what I have subsequently read, on warning humans about environmental damage. They don't want us to damage the Earth beyond repair.

"All of this was transmitted simply by staring into this hybrid baby's eyes. They say the eyes are the gateway to the soul and I feel this for the hybrids also. As I held this child, I also got a sense of a real sadness and a real longing to belong. They were trapped between worlds. The Grey in attendance interrupted and spoke into my mind, 'This is your pod now. You will know them and help them. They will know you and help you.' I was very unsure of the depths of that statement but over the next few years I met and interacted with these children.

"I would often be taken, in between the more gynaecological focused experiences, and would play or sometimes simply spend time just being with these children. Sometimes we would just sit and be with each other. Sometimes they would ask questions. It was always a one-way street, it was always me giving to them.

"Now whether these children were created by my eggs or DNA, I am unsure. But I felt a connection. I am unsure whether it was a genuine connection or whether that feeling was manipulated for me to bond with these children. I especially felt a strong connection as they started to develop into a more teen-like stage or appearance. They were becoming more differentiated. You could almost start to detect some personality traits. But there was always this sense that they were connected to some hive mind, almost as if there was always someone, unseen, whispering in their ear. You can see them become a little vacant temporarily as if they were being told something. It is only for a second, but you can spot when they are connecting with something else.

"Over the years, as they got closer to adulthood as we would understand it, they detached somewhat until one day I was taken aboard and told that I would no longer see them. I was now in my 50's and even though I do not fully understand my relationship with these hybrid children, I still felt I needed to know the outcome of 'the story'. I guess that is a very human need. I never had children of my own due to a lot of gynaecological issues, which I believe originated from my experiences. I had been used for decades as some sort of surrogate parent and now I was being cut off. I fell into a deep depression. I was so depressed about how my life had been impacted and used for reasons unknown and never given any meaningful insights as to what this was all about. Soon after that all my experiences ended. Like I was of no further use to them, so I was cast aside.

"It left a huge hole in my life. That 'not knowing' eats away at me. What was the purpose? Why me? Why was my life impacted in this way with no hints or answers? All those months of crippling menstrual problems and pains, all that emotional effort to connect with those strange hybrids, and for what? I gained so little, and they took so much.

"The isolation is difficult to deal with, also. There are very few people you can talk to. I have tried but unless you know about this phenomena, people will think you are absolutely crazy. Nobody asks for this, and nobody really wants it. But it happens and it will continue to happen. For your typical abductee or experiencer, there is very little agency that they have over their lives. Reading all the books on the subject, which I did a few years after my experiences started, well, it doesn't give you much satisfaction to know this is happening all over the world. There is no comfort in acknowledging other people's pain, in my opinion. Today someone will have an experience they didn't want. Tomorrow it will be someone else. There is no closure in that. I never wanted any of this, but I do want that closure to all my questions. I doubt that will happen. So, I just am left to wonder."

Coming Soon

Testimony - Volume 2: The Group

I was invited to spend a year observing an abductee/experiencer support group based in London.

The intention and messages from the abductors came out in these sessions, loud and clear: The future looks dark and bleak. An Intervention is Here.

ABOUT THE AUTHOR

Andy Russell has been researching the UFO & Abduction phenomena since the mid-1980s. Andy also spends a lot of time utilizing FOIA legislation to push Governments to reveal their knowledge of the UFO phenomena. Andy has appeared on the TV shows "UFO Hunters" and "Ancient Aliens".

Printed in Great Britain
by Amazon